WHERE WE LIVE

WHERE
WE
LIVE

❧

ESSAYS
ABOUT
INDIANA

EDITED BY DAVID HOPPE

INDIANA UNIVERSITY PRESS ❧ BLOOMINGTON AND INDIANAPOLIS

Library of Congress Cataloging-in-Publication Data

Where we live : essays about Indiana / edited by David Hoppe.
p.   cm.
Contents: Landscape and imagination / Scott Russell Sanders—Indiana origin stories / Michael Wilkerson—A muffled humming like the droning of the bees / George Schricker, Jr.—Ethos and creativity / Mari Evans—Hoosier women in a male economy / Teresa Ghilarducci—Living downtown / Michael Martone—Hurry, Mom, the sunset is Up! / Kay Franklin—The literature of place and no place / Wiliam O'Rourke—Impulsive Indiana inspiration / Michael Schelle—Indiana sports / Hal Higdon—On being an old stump / James Alexander Thom—Looking backward / James H. Madison.
ISBN 0-253-32801-2.—ISBN 0-253-20540-9 (pbk.)
1. Indiana—Civilization.   2. Indiana—Social life and customs.
I. Hoppe, David.
F526.5.W48   1989
977.2—dc19   89-2002
                                                                          CIP
2 3 4 5   93 92 91 90 89

CONTENTS

Contents

❦

vi

ACKNOWLEDGMENTS

Thanks for their parts in the realization of this project are due the National Endowment for the Humanities for its continuing support of the work of the Indiana Humanities Council; the Board of the Indiana Humanities Council and the Council's Executive Director, Dr. Kenneth L. Gladish; Eileen Cornelius; and, especially, Marty Minx, whose assistance with the preparation of this manuscript was indispensable.

DRH

INTRODUCTION

DAVID HOPPE

Indiana is changing. This statement, taken by itself, means little. After all, the same might be said of any state in the union. Change, the shifting and remodeling of circumstances and expectations, is probably the dominant characteristic of our time. Indiana is not immune to the momentum of history.

Yet Indiana may be a special case. Few states have taken such a stubborn pride in holding fast to old ways, to resisting trends and standing apart from some of the social and political movements that have, at times, defined and redefined other regions and locales.

Saying that Indiana is changing refers to something more than another temporary incarnation on the spinning wheel of America's boom and bust social landscape. One is talking here about the prospect of real gains, inevitable losses, and uncertainty.

How people orient themselves in such a time—as individuals and as citizens in relationship to a larger community—represents a prime focus of the Indiana Humanities Council. This book is an occasion to further the Council's work; an attempt to better understand where we live and what is happening here at this moment in our state's history.

Decisions now being made in towns, cities, and regions throughout Indiana will likely determine the course of life for decades to come. Opportunities for growth are apparent in all directions. But the social fabric of a place can also be left ragged in the name of progress. In conceiving of this collection of essays, it seemed useful to create an opportunity for a selection of the state's writers, thinkers, and artists to reflect on the experience of living here, to add their perspectives to the continuing discussion about the state's direction and, perhaps, to provoke some additional discussions as well.

The voices you will encounter in this book come from the country, from small towns and cities. They are not intended to be representative in a social science sense; this is not a demographer's cross-section. Nor do the writers here mean for theirs to be the last word on whatever subject they take in hand. Just the opposite: in every case the hope is that these pieces will prompt questions, encourage reflection, and spark the kind of talk that might make a difference in how people regard themselves and the communities of which they are a part.

Contributors to this collection were asked to write about Indiana from a personal standpoint. And while the underlying intention was not necessarily the creation of a systematic overview of the state, a composite portrait does begin to emerge. We should be surprised neither by the complexity of the image that presents itself nor that the Hoosier stereotype—rustic, suspicious, and naive—appears so shopworn by comparison.

It is, perhaps, a measure of Indiana's changing climate that the women and men you will encounter in these pages are independently yet consistently concerned not with the state as an insular unit in need of celebration, but with ways of seeing who and where they are; with the cultivation of that sensibility which makes the life of quality possible.

Certain themes trace themselves through this collection like the wood grain patterns of an oak tabletop. In these pieces there are concerns with how we look at history and the legacy of the past; the uneasy relationship between creativity and time-honored value systems; the needs for subtlety and humility as we approach our landscape and each other. These are, of course, matters of universal significance. The ground we attend to here, however, is Indiana.

One rarely knows the extent or degree to which ideas, offered freely, have impact. Too often our society seems allergic to ideas, preferring attitudes— ready-to-wear and easily discarded—instead. In spite of this, experience demonstrates that in the right place, at the right time, an idea can make a difference, actually change a life. Ideas about where we live are in this book.

WHERE WE LIVE

❦ Scott Russell Sanders

LANDSCAPE AND IMAGINATION

TO BE intimate with a landscape is to know its moods and contours as you would know a lover's. The shape of breasts and hills, the sound of a laugh or the song of bullfrogs, the smell of hair and honeysuckle—such knowledge becomes part of who you are. As in marriage, however, what is utterly familiar may lose its charm, may in fact become invisible, until you are deprived of it. Absent yourself a while from lover or landscape, and upon returning you will recognize with fresh acuity what you had known but forgotten.

I experienced such a freshening of awareness not long ago, when I returned with my family to Indiana after a year's sojourn in Boston. We drove into the state one afternoon toward the end of July, the air rushing in our car windows like the breath from a furnace, a haze of muggy heat blurring the flat horizon. Thunderheads were massing in the west, grave clouds that cast their dark temper onto the whole countryside. A rising wind made silver maples show the pale undersides of their leaves and set cattails stirring in stock ponds and bent the trajectories of birds. After a year in the bunched-up terrain of New England, I was amazed by the extent of sky, the openness of the land, the vigor of the head-high corn, the loneliness of the farmsteads, the authority of those clouds. . . .

We pulled over and shut off the engine for a change of drivers. I could smell hot tar bubbling in the joints of the road, creosote in telephone poles, windblown dust from cultivated fields, the mustiness of new-mown hay, the green pungency of Queen Anne's lace and chicory and black-eyed Susans. In the stillness I could hear the distant grumble of thunder like a clearing of throats, and the nearby ratcheting of crickets and cicadas. Only when I caught those smells, heard those sounds, did I realize how much I had missed them in the East, just as I had missed the sight of a level horizon broken by power lines, grain elevators, water towers, silos, and the shade trees around farmhouses. During our absence, the Midwest had suffered through a plague of cicadas. When we had called Indiana from Boston, the ruckus of insects over the telephone had all but drowned out the voices of our friends. Now, as I walked around to the passenger side of the car, cast-off cicada shells crunched under my feet. That sensation also was a rediscovery.

We angled south from Indianapolis toward home in Bloomington, coasting down from the glacial plain into wooded hills, a landscape not so dramatically different from that of New England. And yet even here my heightened senses picked up a hundred details that characterize this place: the white flare of sycamores in creekbeds, limestone roadcuts, pastures growing up in cedar and sumac, bottom lands planted in soybeans, sway-backed barns carrying advertisements for chewing tobacco on their flanks, sinuous gravel driveways leading to basketball hoops, shacks and trailers interspersed with sprawling ranch houses, the occasional white clapboard house as fancy with filigree and as big as a steamboat, the clutter of billboards (outlawed in most of New England), the low-slung evangelical churches, and over it all that sovereign sky. The light was the silken yellow peculiar to a region of tornadoes. The fields recently harrowed were the color of buckskin. Unchecked by ocean or mountains, the storm that came roaring through the hills was another local species, its thunder shaking us inside the car with sudden jolting changes in air pressure. In the twilight before the deluge, fireflies along the roadside blinked their semaphore of desire. Even in the dark that overtook us before we reached our front door, there was an unmistakable familiarity in the roasted-earth smell of rain and in the leap of lightning, which lit up the swirling treetops and shaggy hills.

The effects of my year away have not yet worn off. The landscape of the Midwest, familiar to me since childhood, still wears an air of novelty. T. S. Eliot spoke of such a renewal of vision in those magisterial lines from *The Four Quartets*:

> We shall not cease from exploration
> And the end of all our exploring
> Will be to arrive where we started
> And know the place for the first time.

It is increasingly rare for any of us to know with passion and subtlety a particular place, whether a town or a state or a region. We have itchy feet. Once every five years, on average, we pull up stakes and move. No sooner do we arrive somewhere than we begin hankering for a new spot that's richer, more lively, more celebrated. Most of the time we huddle indoors, gazing at magazine pages and television screens that benumb us, no matter where we live, with the same uprooted images. When we do venture outside, we barrel along superhighways that have been designed to ignore the terrain, past a blur of franchise joints, or we glide through corridors above the clouds.

Bothered by this, wishing to know the place where I have been set down, I drive the back roads of Indiana, tramp across country, wade the streams, look about. It is never a simple matter actually to see what is before your eyes. You notice what memory and knowledge and imagination have prepared you to see. I take pleasure in silos, for example—the antique masonry ones covered by domed roofs, the squat silver ones wearing conical caps, the giant blue steel ones bristling with chutes—partly because their vertical strokes are a dramatic calligraphy above the horizon, partly because, as a boy, I spent many hours loading chopped cornstalks into the silo of a dairy farm and many hours more, half dizzy from the yeasty smell, pitching fermented silage to cows. As a teenager I also helped make hay and build houses, so there is beauty for me in a meadow of alfalfa freshly cut and raked into windrows, or a field humped with great round bales, or a pile of lumber beside a raw foundation, or the flash of a hammer in sunlight. My muscles know the ache and grace in such things. Likewise, for reasons of memory, I pay attention to all manner of barns, the venerable ones with boards missing as well as the brand spanking new ones. Admiring lone maples and oaks in pastures, their winter branches a net of nerves against the sky, their summer shade a haven for horses, I remember climbing such trees. Memory compels me to stop on railroad tracks and gaze down their latticed miles, to survey the junked cars and tractors and combines rusting in weed-grown ditches, to linger on the main streets of drowsy towns where clocks run slowly, to follow the inky flight of crows against a snow-covered hillside or the lope of a stray dog along a ridge. What I see is stitched through and through with my own past.

What I see when I look at the land is also informed by the company I have kept, beginning with that of my parents. Reared on a Mississippi farm, my father loved to poke about the countryside, studying crops and fences, eyeing the livestock. He would speculate on the quality of soil, squeezing a handful to judge the amount of clay, sniffing it, tasting a pinch. He wondered aloud about the facts of ownership and debt, since land took on meaning for him as property. A connoisseur of carpentry, he remarked with equal pleasure on weather-gray outhouses and gingerbread mansions. He counted the cross-bars on telephone poles, by way of estimating the density of rural conversations. He would stop to shoot the breeze with idlers at gas stations and feed stores and doughnut cafes, wherever men with time on their hands gossiped about planting and harvest. He avoided cities, because little grew there aside from people, so much of the dirt had been paved, and because in cities he could not see, as he could on farms, the fruits of a family's or an individual's labor and skill. My father had little use for scenery, and not much taste for nature in the raw. The land he cared for had been lived in, worked on, made over to fit human designs.

My mother, by contrast, is a city person with an artist's eye for texture and composition, and she goes to the country as to a feast for the senses. She notices every flower in bloom, the silhouettes of trees, the delicate tracery of hills, the architecture of clouds, the effects of light. What people have done to the land interests her less than what nature has done and is doing. My father's nose was ruined by smoking and boxing, but my mother more than makes up for it with a sense of smell that can detect lilacs or pigs from implausible distances. She can distinguish and name a hundred colors, many of them derived from oil-paints, such as burnt sienna and raw umber. She can discern the slightest change in texture, as though the earth were a bolt of cloth over which she glides a subtle hand.

I learned what to notice and value in the landscape from both my parents, at first unconsciously and then deliberately. Like my mother, I exult in the non-stop show that nature puts on, the play of light and shade, the chorus of birdsong and running water and wind-shaken trees, the seasons, the plant's voluptuous curves, and the infinite palette of paints. Like my father, I also relish the long-running human show, the fields cleared of stones, farmhouses built to capture sunlight and breezes, groves of walnuts planted as a legacy for grandchildren, high-tension lines, corn-cribs, orchards, bridges, anything that testifies to sweat and ingenuity and care. Between them, my parents taught me to honor whatever has been handsomely accomplished on the surface of the earth, whether by nature or by nature's offspring, us.

Like all landscapes, that of Indiana is a palimpsest, written over by centuries of human scrawls and by millennia of natural ones. Every fence, highway, billboard, and clearing is an utterance, more or less eloquent, more or less durable. You can see, for example, in the checkerboard layout of crops and the right-angle turns of local roads the marks of a surveying grid that was imposed on all the country north and west of the Ohio River by the Land Ordinance of 1785. It was an unprecedented gesture, a Newtonian abstraction, reflecting the Enlightenment belief in reason, to ignore nature's own contours and inscribe on the land a uniform pattern of mile-square boxes. The map of the Midwest came to resemble graph paper, each block of which, in keeping with Jeffersonian ideals, was to support a citizen-farmer. The grid encouraged the establishment of isolated, self-sufficient homesteads, in contrast to the village culture of New England or the plantation culture of the South. During the period of settlement, what one did on his or her property was private business, and it remains largely private to this day, which is why zoning boards and planning commissions have such a hard time here, and why in many places the Indiana countryside is a hodgepodge of contradictory visions: grain fields alternating with strip mines, stretches of woods interrupted by used-car lots, dumps in ferny ravines, trailer courts in the middle of meadows, gas stations and motels plopped down wherever the traffic flows thickly enough. In much of Indiana, the isolated freeholdings have gradually been combined into larger and larger parcels, the remnants of forest have been cut down, the hedge rows cleared, the meandering creeks straightened, the swampy lowlands drained, thus further rationalizing the landscape, pushing it toward an industrial ideal of profitable uniformity.

Native creatures inscribe their own messages on the landscape, messages that one can learn, however imperfectly, to read. Deer trails mark out subtle changes in slope. The population of butterflies and owls and hawks is a measure of how much poison we have been using; the abundance of algae in ponds is a measure of our fertilizer use. The condition of trees is a gauge of the acidity in rain. Merely finding out the name and history of a plant may deepen one's awareness of a place. For years I had admired the coppery grass that grows in knee-high tufts along Indiana's roadsides before I discovered that it is called little bluestem, a survivor from the prairies. Now I admire those luminous grasses with new pleasure, for I see them as visitors from a wild past.

I also know from books that, except for dunes and prairies and swamps near Lake Michigan, all of what would become Indiana was dense with forest when the first white settlers arrived. This means that almost every acre of soybeans and corn represents an acre of trees cut down, stumps pulled out or left to rot: oak and beech, hickory and maple, dogwood, sassafras, buckeye, elm, tulip poplar, ash. In two centuries, a mere eyeblink in the long saga of the planet, Indiana has been transformed from a wilderness dotted by human clearings to a human landscape dotted by scraps of wilderness. Today, only the southern third of Indiana is heavily wooded, but the speed with which redbud and locust and cedars march into abandoned pastures convinces me that the entire state, left to itself, would slip back into forest again within a few decades. The highways, untraveled, would succumb to grass. The barns and houses, unroofed, would succumb to rain. It does not trouble me to see our clearings as ephemeral, our constructions as perishable, for that is the fate of all human writing, whether on paper or on earth.

Despite our centuries of scrawling on the landscape, we can still read the deeper marks left by nature—especially, in Indiana, the work of water and ice. For millions of years, while the Appalachians were being uplifted to the east and the Rockies to the west, the land that would become Indiana was forming grain-by-grain in the bed of an ancient ocean, as limestone, siltstone, sandstone, dolomite, shale, slate. It was and remains a placid region, at the core of the continental plate. These sedimentary rocks have never been folded, never heaved up into mountains nor deeply buried and cooked into granite or marble, never burst by volcanoes. When the waters receded, the bedrock, exposed to wind and rain, was carved into low hills. Beginning roughly a million years ago and ending some ten thousand years ago, glaciers bulldozed down from the north, flattening the hills and filling the valleys and burying much of the Midwest beneath a fertile layer of dust and pulverized rock. In their retreat, the glaciers gouged out the stony bed of the Great Lakes and filled them with water, altered the flow of rivers, and left behind a trail of gravel and sand. In Indiana, only a thumb-shaped area stretching about a hundred miles north from the Ohio River escaped the glaciers. The limestone exposed there is laced with caves and underground rivers, pockmarked by sinkholes. Knowing even this much geological history, I look at the flat expanses of black loam, or the polished quartz in a creekbed, or the strata of shale in a bluff with a chastening sense of nature's slow rhythms and our hasty ones.

Without these lessons in seeing, from people and memories and books, the landscape would appear to me as little more than a straggle of postcards.

In fact, without benefit of instruction, in a territory as unglamorous as the Midwest I would probably fail to appreciate even the two-dimensional postcard views. Of all the regions in America, this one has inspired, I would guess, the least smugness from local people and the least rapture from travelers. People do not move here for the scenery. I have no way of checking, but I would venture that fewer landscape snapshots are taken per square mile in the Midwest than in any other part of the country, including the deserts. Millions of people drive through Indiana every year without lifting their gaze from the highway. Those who do glance aside from the line of motion tend to see only indistinguishable fields and humble hills.

I have spent enough time in the mountains of Oregon and Tennessee, the redwood forests of California, the mesa country of New Mexico, the moss-festooned bayous of Louisiana, and along the stony coast of Maine to know the pleasures of spectacular landscapes. How could anyone equipped with nerves fail to rejoice in such places? On the other hand, to know the pleasures of an unspectacular landscape, such as that of Indiana, requires an uncommon degree of attentiveness and insight. It requires one to open wide all the doors of perception. It demands an effort of imagination, by which I mean not what the Romantics meant, a projection of the self onto the world, but rather a seeing of what is already there, in the actual world. I don't claim to possess the necessary wisdom or subtlety, but I aspire to, and I work at it.

Many of those who preceded us in this place were so bent on changing the land to suit their needs that they scarcely looked at what was native. We have only recently begun to realize how much was lost in that refusal to look. Those who preceded us here found an astonishing wealth, not only in lumber and loam and oil, but in the intricacy and beauty of life. Yet they valued almost exclusively what could be used or sold. Generations of settlers treated the land as a storehouse, to be ransacked before moving on. The fact that we dislodged Indians from their home grounds and herded them onto reservations a thousand miles away reveals how little our ancestors valued the sacred connection between a people and a landscape. We are still suffering from the Puritan habit of regarding wild nature as demonic, a realm to be conquered and saved from the Devil. The secular version of this view treats land as raw material for profit; whatever does not yield a return in dollars stands in need of "development," which is an economic form of salvation. Thus a chorus of angry voices cries down every proposal for the creation of wilderness areas or the preservation of wetlands or even for restrictions on the clear-cutting of trees.

Insofar as we are nomads, adrift over the earth and oblivious to its rhythms, we cease to acknowledge the fecund mystery that sustains our existence. We take inordinate pride in our own doings. Acting without regard for the effects our lives will have upon a place, we become dangerous, to ourselves and our descendants. If our own senses fail to teach us, then disasters will, that the land is not merely a backdrop for the human play, not merely a source of raw materials, but is the living skin of the earth. Through this skin we apprehend a being that is alien, a life unfathomable and uncontrollable, and at the same time a being that is kindred, flesh of our flesh.

It is a spiritual discipline to root the mind in a particular landscape, to know it not as a visitor with a camera but as a resident, as one more local creature alongside the red-tailed hawks and sycamores and raccoons. The explorations from which we return to see our home ground afresh may be physical ones, such as my family's sojourn in New England, or they may be journeys of the mind, such as those we take through stories and photographs and paintings. By renewing our vision of the land, we rediscover where it is we truly dwell. Whatever the place we inhabit, we must invest ourselves there with our full powers of awareness if we are to live responsibly, alertly, wisely.

❦ Michael Wilkerson

INDIANA ORIGIN STORIES

WHEN I was twelve or thirteen, I was watching *Jeopardy* after school one day. The game was close; the contestants were sharp, and I liked trying to keep score along with them. Someday, I thought, I would go on game shows and win lots of Hollywood money. The questions weren't that hard. The three men (I recall that they were all men that day) placed their Final Jeopardy bets on the category "Geography." Art Fleming read the question: "What is the 'Hoosier State'?" The camera panned all three contestants. Tortured expressions. Scrawlings. Crossouts. Slamming shut and placing of the little message boards. Sheepish unveilings of the answers: "What is Kansas?" "uh, Art, what is South Dakota?" Finally, the Champion's vain attempt: Missouri.

No, Art said, woeful, benign, so reassuring that, had he not been hired by *Jeopardy*, he could have directed a funeral home: "I'm sorry, the answer is, 'What is Indiana?'"

What is Indiana? Like all tough questions, it needs careful examination. It's hard to explain who we are to folks from other states, just as, within Indiana, I have always had trouble convincing others that my family was probably its happiest in Terre Haute. We lived there in the late 1960s and early 1970s, and our house was a wonder, both to see and to live in: a ramshackle, two-story brick structure from 1824, it had been a mill owner's retreat, a granary when it fell into disrepair, and, it was said (and corroborated by a few feet of collapsed tunnel in the basement), a stop on the Underground Railroad. We had our first color TV in the dining room with its fourteen-foot ceiling and hand-hewn, square-nailed poplar floor. We lived just a mile or so from U.S. Highway 41 and maybe five miles from U.S. 40, which ran east-west and bisected the city. In and around Terre Haute—within bicycling distance—was everything that mattered: an early regional shopping mall, an old strip mine that had been converted to a park, a motel pool where I had a membership, a bargain outlet for donuts and Hostess Fruit Pies, the exotic, slumping Syrian Grocery where a boy could pick up real fireworks, seemingly endless fields, woods, and creeks, and the city golf course where I could play all summer for twenty-five of my parents' dollars.

When I wanted to explore more sinister worlds, just down the road was the huge federal prison, where many of my friends' fathers worked (every once in a while the family would huddle indoors while prison officials and deputies prowled our woods for an escapee); across the road from what would later become my high school, separated only by a fence, was the Father Gibault School for Boys, which later became famous as the institution that tried to civilize young Charles Manson. Sometimes at night we could smell the by-products of one of the local chemical factories, where, the older boys said, they made napalm.

Terre Haute was the center of the world, and if I needed any further proof, all I had to do was listen to the endless civic boosterism on radio and television. The Chamber of Commerce called it "Pride City." If Indiana was the "Crossroads of America," then Terre Haute, despite not being centrally located, had to be the state's soul, since the intersection of U.S. 40 (the old National Road) and U.S. 41—the literal Crossroads—was right downtown, at the courthouse.

What is Indiana. My Terre Haute is as particular as anyone's childhood home; it can only provide one small set of clues to a mystery that may not have a single answer. I still look for ways to solve the riddle, which permeates most of my writing and much of my thought. Pieces of information arrive in unexpected ways: when I lived in Baltimore, I first heard, from a writer who'd strayed from his research about the colonial-era Poet Laureate of Maryland, that Indiana was nearly named Tecumseh by the Territorial Legislature. "Land of the Indians" was settled upon as a compromise. I can imagine the legislative dickering: "Yes, we should honor the particular population in question, but to single out any one heathen individual would simply be too provocative."

I've long suspected that to the Indians, the state was more of a Crossroads of America than they would have liked. At 4-H camps, we used to divide ourselves into squads named after tribes that had inhabited Indiana. We had a slew of names to choose from: Wea, Potawatomi, Sioux, Wyandottes, Iroquois, Miami, even Seminole. They all passed through here, some staying longer than others, few able to claim the land even for a generation, none holding on long enough to be granted a reservation, all now far away. Thus, we live in a state named after something it doesn't have; we who occupy the land now may not have invented the "Land of the Indians" slogan, but we live with its lie, somewhere deep in our minds.

Our collective unconscious may be shot full of Indiana origin stories: for example, how the federal government carved Ohio out of the old Northwest Territory, leaving the rest as the Indiana Territory. Once, we had dominion over Michigan, Illinois, and most of Wisconsin. How did "Indiana" end up as the smallest chunk? How'd those other states get the Great Lakes, the virgin pine forests, the glacial spring water? Like everyone else in my generation, I took Indiana History in fourth grade. It's a rude thing to learn not only that your state is unknown elsewhere, but also that "they" or "the government" took away most of your territory long before even your grandfather was born. Instead of a "Big Bang" theory of creation, Indiana's is one of being whittled away.

In the spring of 1987, *Harpers* published one of its occasional United States maps. Some of these show climates, others electoral votes; this one charted the dominant religions of the country. To be dominant, a religion needed to have more adherents than any other in the area, and at least 25 percent of the population. Catholics were blue, Lutherans green, Baptists brown, and so on. Only two areas of the entire country were left the blank white of the empty page, with no faith dominant: eastern Oregon's desert, which God himself may never have seen, and southern Indiana. It made me think of all those wonderful, rotting little towns where there may be a different church for every twelve inhabitants. What, really, are the key differences between the Pentecostals and the Apostolics? Yet sometimes you can see their chapels, less than a block apart, structures crumbling, paint peeling for lack of members. In other cases, these tiny churches might be the only new buildings in an entire town. In certain sections of Indiana, you can find the Amish and Mennonites, some incarnations of which won't tolerate any motor vehicles, others which will accept only black cars, still others with restrictions on two-tones, radios, etc. Do you cover your TV when the Brethren visit, or are you allowed one at all? If you raise tobacco, can you join the Church, or are you merely permitted to contribute money and attend services as one of the Unsaved?

Such differences seem obscure to me, but beyond the narrow sectarianism of small-town, southern Indiana, there are real ethnic and cultural schisms. It's a state where a town whose street signs are still in German can be twelve miles away from one named after an English county, where the Abbey can sit alongside the Pilgrim Holiness Church, or, most bizarre of all, where a bandbox country chapel with spangles on the ceiling, a blue and hot pink neon cross on the altar, and a satellite dish in the yard can be directly across the road from the only Tibetan *stupa* in the United States.

What is Indiana? Perhaps no one is so perennially vexed over this question as the folks in Indianapolis who, once every four years or so, have to design a new license plate. We'd have all the money we need if the state could only collect a nickel for every time a Hoosier has been asked, "Why do you have 'Wander' on your car?"

I was relieved along with everyone else when Wander's time was up. "Back Home Again" isn't too bad, but I'm wary: it may have set a popular-song precedent that will lead to "On the Banks of the Wabash" or even "Indiana Wants Me" on our next couple of plates. From murky, indecipherable drawings of George Rogers Clark traipsing toward Vincennes, through Wander and now onto a plate that conjures up the guy who played Gomer Pyle, we clearly have not found the Hoosier equivalent of "America's Dairyland," "The Bluegrass State," or even "Famous Potatoes." Those are real, tangible images. Our challenge is greater: to find something non-physical. "Land of Enchantment," à la New Mexico? It obviously doesn't fit. Our most recent license plate is the result of a competition in which 891 happy Hoosiers sent in their nominees. The three finalists: "Hoosier Heartland," "Feel at Home," and "The Hoosier State." All these lack any concrete sense of how we differ from other states, but at least they don't take the goofy risks of "Wander."

In asking friends and family for their thoughts on living in Indiana, I discovered that one thing Hoosiers like to do is what I'm up to here: the License Plate Game. "49th in State Services." "Millions for Prisons, Nothing for Education." "No Damned Democrats Here." "We'll Pay You to Put Your Factory in Indiana." "A Place to Be From." "Gateway to Ohio." One friend proposed a pictorial plate showing a house trailer, a satellite dish, and a car up on blocks in the front yard. Another suggested, "Through Wandering."

To be fair, in an era when the world is jammed with Disney Worlds and touristy meccas full of overpriced, prepared "fun," to Wander is not inherently a bad thing. Once I was Wandering (before I knew it was something the state wanted me to do) in Hoosier National Forest along a cliffside trail. Climbing over a huge rock, I grabbed a sturdy-looking five-inch tree trunk to pull myself up. Somehow, it had died, weathered, and stayed in place for who knows how many years, until it crumbled into powder in my hand. When had the last human walked there? Now that's Wandering.

The most obvious thing to put on the license plate is finalist number three: "The Hoosier State." But I bet the folks in Indianapolis who came up with "Wander" either had their consciousnesses shaped by *Jeopardy* or also wished for a nickel every time someone asked them the origin of the nickname. I remember in my college days the multiple attempts of Indiana University to make the word into flesh. The Athletic Department wanted a mascot; since we weren't the Wildcats or the Bulldogs, the University left it open to the world to define "Hoosier." For a while, there was a guy in a giant buffalo head, perhaps continuing the tradition of representing the state by what it no longer contains. Fans booed the buffalo head, along with the bumbling IU football team. Next came Hoosier Dan, an oversized country bumpkin in overalls with a plastic head complete with polystyrene freckles. Hoosier Dan got booed, too, and justifiably so. After all, Indiana is a small state, thirty-eighth of the fifty in land mass, but something like fourteenth in population. We're mostly urban, and our college students are paying several thousand dollars a year not to end up looking like Hoosier Dan. Today Hoosier Dan has gone where all the "Wander" plates and buffalo heads have gone, and the team wins without a mascot.

What in the world is a Hoosier? One of the first things that must happen to non-natives who move here is experiencing the telling of the Possible Explanations of How We Got Our Nickname. Was it the pioneers, visiting each other's far-sprawling cabins, crying, "Hello . . . Who's 'ere?" Or was it the riverboat captain John Hoosier who gave us our name? Or, my favorite, that early Hoosiers were so tough they routinely got into knife fights, and it was customary to look at the floor of a cabin or early bar and ask, "Whose ear?" Maybe they should have made Hoosier Dan earless, wearing a boat captain's hat. Who are we?

In editing an anthology of contemporary fiction about Indiana, I was struck by a recurring vision the writers expressed, of Indiana as a landscape filled with alternately grotesque and wise old-timers, who both terrify and educate their wayward yuppie grandchildren from the city (usually Indianapolis). Few writers seemed interested in presenting stories about what it's really like to live in Indianapolis, or Muncie, or Terre Haute; though most lived in cities, their stories were rural, generally bleak, often looking into the distant past for any sense of hope or redemption.

One writer described his forlorn character as "a Hoosier without a who." Perhaps in that one line he'd stumbled onto the nagging problem. Indiana is basketball, yes, and woods and empty factories and chicken packers and tomato pickers and John Cougar Mellencamp's farm-foreclosed landscapes; it's boarded-up downtowns and railroads now become bike paths; it's mobile homes, added onto and aluminum-porched and barbecue-grilled and satellite-dished until they almost look like real houses. If there was a common thread, when our better writers took a hard look at Hoosier living, they seemed to find a tight-lipped people, afraid to take risks but longing to leave, just trying to hang on in a tough world. Trucks didn't run well and neighbors were as likely to shoot you as lend you a cup of sugar. In one story, a man goes to his Amish neighbors to buy a part for his tractor, hating their kind all the way down and back, but dealing with them anyway, after all his other options had run out.

In many cases, I thought our would-be contributors, perhaps non-native Hoosiers (our curious system of academe ensures that almost no native writer will ever hold a teaching job at an Indiana college or university), were a little smug, somewhat thoughtlessly superior and superficial about the real Indiana. If not that, they tried too hard and without authenticity to be pastoral. Perhaps I should accept the majority vote of those who sent stories as accurate, not at all misguided: we are urban demographically, but rural psychologically. Remodeling the Indiana Repertory Theater and luring the Colts from Baltimore haven't really changed the fundamental character (and charm) of Indianapolis, which, when I was growing up, was always referred to as "the biggest small town in America."

I keep coming back to the small town, the manageable chunk of Terre Haute that was my youth, the Trafalgar my father's side comes from, the Franklin where my mother's side lives. We're protected there, from all the dangers we can and cannot name. I think of my mother-in-law, the archetypal queen of safety, who once asserted that if my wife and I continued to swim in the local lake the snapping turtles there would "take our legs off." In a more literary way, I don't think it's an accident that Michael Martone's recent book *Safety Patrol* is a collection of Hoosier stories about the fear of danger. Perhaps the failure of the statewide canal system, which, as every fourth grader learns, bankrupted the state in the mid-nineteenth century, is imprinted upon us: don't take risks.

Maybe we need yet another license plate: "Land of Timidity." It's an idea that expresses itself in our speech, or lack of it. I can't begin to count the number of times I've attended family reunions, of both my relatives and my wife's, to spend most of the day watching football or trying not to reveal anything. We are as curtailed of tongue as Northeasterners are unstoppable. In a way, our silence is honorable and good; we don't want to bother others with our problems, which are probably just like theirs, and our mundane news. We know they don't want to hear it. But our silence also means that we don't think there's much good in analysis, in synthesis, in fact that there may not be anything much to talk about.

The world goes on, and it does what it does, without our help or control. Perhaps that's connected to the longtime Hoosier hatred of Government. Ever since I lived in Wisconsin, which posits a governmental solution to virtually every problem, and which is characterized by slogans like "Forward," and "The Progressive Ideal," I've been struck by Indiana as the Land of Anarchy.

Another license plate slogan? Whichever party's in power, we don't want regulation, interference, or even much legislation. Our state identity expresses itself more clearly in our reluctance to give money to the government (we are forty-seventh in tax effort relative to state wealth) than in any other area. We are quiet, going our own way, understating both our problems and our achievements—to toot one's own horn seems un-Hoosier. We are, quintessentially, small town.

In the small town, we don't see the hand of government; all we need from it is a couple of firemen (though we hope to get by with volunteers) and a post office that delivers once a day. Hoosiers are often said to be anti-education, but I think we are more opposed to the loquaciousness and worldliness, the focused ambition and sense of self, that you get along the way to a college degree. We know that our children will leave us if they get too much learning; there's no niche for a poet or a microbiologist, either in the actual small town or the idealized small town of the Indiana psyche.

The ultimate Hoosier goal, overriding all the state's and big business's talk about global economies, economic development, and interconnectedness in a shrinking world, is to stay put, to find, maintain, or rediscover that Indiana of the heart that may not be physically present, but that lives on within us. Since I was a small child, I've been indoctrinated by the family creation myth of How the Family Came to Indiana. My Great-Grandma Walker, who died in 1975 after 98 years, went west with her family in the 1880s in a covered wagon. Like many would-be pioneers, they faced pestilence, battle, weather, unfamiliar landscapes, disaster. Shortly after she reached Kansas City, her father died, and the survivors turned their backs on the Great Plains, the Rockies, the unseen Sierras, and headed home to Brown County. My wife's relatives have singled out and often retell a similar tale about one of her ancestors.

I had eight great-grandparents, but Grandma Walker is the one I always hear about, the archetypal Hoosier; she did as I would do a hundred years later when I left Wisconsin, and as so many of the contributors to our fiction anthology responded when called upon to produce a contemporary vision of Indiana. After nearly two hundred years as a state, we are still like my great-grandmother in the covered wagon: defined and maybe predestined by our origin stories, always turning back.

❦ George Schricker, Jr.

A MUFFLED HUMMING LIKE THE
DRONING OF THE BEES

IT IS hot in the second story of this old building in downtown Plymouth, Indiana, and the fan blows across the scattered papers on my desk and gives their edges life. Outside, on the main street below, people are yelling, laughing, and carousing. Some of them are school age and are howling their last caterwauls of summer before the bell rings and their work begins. Some are older and howl out the frustrations of repetitive factory work that leaves them bleary-eyed and hollow. Some swill alcohol from pop cans, while others clandestinely exchange drugs. To further fuel this scene there is an endless parade of vehicles: motorcycles, jacked-up four-wheel-drive trucks, rusting-out junk heaps patched with spray paint, and shiny new sports cars. Many of their drivers will test their explosively loud mufflers, listening to them career and echo in this century-old canyon of brick and mortar which lines old Highway 31 at its Yellow River crossing. I know this noise well. It shoots into my front office like ear-driven spikes full of steel and anger. My head aches from so much sound. What a cacophony of squealing and screeching and cursing. And, in addition, if I look below, I see the visual noise of broken glass, discarded wrappers, half-empty and distended soda pop cans, crumpled plastic and paper bags—all dutifully swept into dust pans by the early morning shopkeepers.

This year the chaos seems worse than ever. Perhaps because I have grown less able to cope with its cumulative effect. Or perhaps because new benches line the downtown sidewalks like invitational gestures no adolescent-minded person can resist. Regardless, I do feel now, after living here for ten years, that there is something more to all of this than just what one may witness by walking to the window. The very brokenness of the picture haunts me, like the limbs torn and dangling from the newly planted trees below. Something runs deep here, beneath the noise, destruction, and disrespect for others; its significance flashes and spins like a glimmering trout that has just taken the line. Here, high above the kiva of this madcap circuitous ritual, I am caught by the dark mythos contained in this play of futility and malaise, immersed in its innocence as a symbol and cast adrift by its meaning.

This is the hottest summer I can ever remember. Just living in it is oppressive, my bare back sticking firmly to the old Naugahyde office chair. I am reminded daily that something is profoundly amiss about this particular heat. It is said to be a global problem. *Time*, *Newsweek*, and the network news have sanctioned this "new" phenomenon of 1988 with intense pictorial coverage. Even Big Brother's own scientists have confirmed it—the drought is here. What's worse, it is here to stay.

Desertification of vast areas of Canada and the U.S. is likely to occur. Groundwater levels will drop. Good water will become scarce. The protective ozone layer of the earth is being eaten away by an overabundance of fossil-fueled noxious gas and refrigerant chlorofluorocarbons. The rapid destruction of our forests and much of our greenspace worldwide has added to the problem. The "greenhouse effect" is *real*. And once again (à la nuclear holocaust) the possibility for our self-destruction is made evident.

How, I reflect, do these seemingly separate events (the disrespect for public community and property by our youth and the global catastrophe brewing in the upper atmosphere) mirror the same reality? How do they speak of a mutually destructive tendency evidenced in our culture's history and its lack of respect for its own children? And how might we begin to overcome the inertia of such a force, begin to break it of its will, in the interest of preserving our children's future?

The Native Americans, or Anishnabee (meaning: human being), as many prefer to be called, are a good example here. For thousands of years they took an active part in caring for the earth and all its creatures. They viewed man as not the most intelligent of the animal kingdom, but the least intelligent. They were a proud people, but they knew humbleness of spirit as well. They were very aware that human beings were full of darkness, because they could view it in their own lives. Their stories mirrored this awareness. Particularly the Coyote, Witsga, Nanaboso, and Nebush stories were full of such lessons. Coyote, the Trickster, was half-god/animal and half-fallen human, and it was that human part which was always getting him into trouble. In these stories one is led to the humble truth: humans are the only animals that ever forget their "instructions." All the other animals remember through their instincts the instructions sent from the Great Spirit, while humankind is forever being led astray.

It is out of this recognition of humankind's innate stupidity and perpetual state of unknowing that the Native Americans developed a strong tradition of reverence for all animals, looking to them as signs of the Great Spirit's incarnate wisdom. From this awareness the Native American culture developed and continued, surviving through incredible hardships on this continent and maintaining much of its cultural identity in a philosophical and spiritual sense, even to the present day.

It is a short step from seeing God's spirit revealed in the animals, to seeing it revealed inside of everything on which animals depend. Indeed, for Native Americans, the trees, the rocks, the plants, the air, and all the land reveal the very nature of the creator. None of these was inanimate, dead, or soulless. For this reason, the Anishnabee could not own, use, or destroy anything wantonly without invoking the shame of the tribe. Prayers were offered for those things which they needed for their survival and the accumulation of property was viewed as an ignorant and selfish act. With this understanding, Native Americans built a culture with a very strong sense of place that included a vast holistic knowledge system of all its many inhabitants. This corpus of knowledge guided them through the sensitive art of caretaking, noting particular changes within the environment which might describe excesses, altering their behavior as a result. Within this habit of humility and its ensuing watchfulness, they developed a great tradition, along with all primal peoples, of a deeply rooted earth stewardship, a stewardship that grounded each individual within a tribal community collateral and intermeshed with the surrounding landscape.

It is within this context that I wish to situate our two earlier-mentioned events: one being the ever-growing disrespect of young people for public space and property, and the other being the eminent global debacle of the "greenhouse effect," readying itself for the destruction of our ecosphere. Both of these events mirror, at bottom, the same degree of unawareness. They are steeped in our inability, as a culture and as a people, to see and perhaps more importantly to feel the place we all live in as *sacred*. In a thousand ways, both of these examples are born from countless daily rituals that desecrate the wholeness of our living environment. And what is more, these rituals work to sever each succeeding generation further from the truth of our interdependence with our surrounding habitat. Viewed from this perspective, each act of neglect and assault within one context is but a reflection of a larger symptomatic trend. Bottles lining our sidewalks and roadways are symbols of our burgeoning landfills and our penchant for speed and convenience regardless of spiritual costs. Swearing and cursing and yelling and noisemaking of all kinds are reactions from people whose souls and senses have been smothered and dulled by the drone of television, radios, and motorized transport. People march to the beat of alarms, bells, sirens, and loudspeakers while simultaneously shutting out and covering up the music of crickets, birds, and the wind in the trees. Graffiti and other various acts of vandalism reflect a culture reeling from the overload of advertising jingles, billboards, and telephone hucksters drowning out the very possibility for silence, solitude, and self-reflection.

In almost every aspect of their behavior, the youth in this endless parade of effrontery react with uncanny precision to the unreasoned destructiveness of their personal environment with more of the same. They thumb their noses at the pretensions of public pride and property, built on our communities' urge for a fascist control and manipulation of the environment. It is as if, as humankind builds for itself an increasingly artificial environment, its disempowered members act more overtly to express our avarice through public display. Although seemingly unconscious, their actions symbolize a disturbing agenda—an agenda of egocentricity which, like a drug, has hooked our culture on a path of escapism and is sending it on an increasingly desacralizing spiral, which through its retreat from its own inner darkness is, in essence, anti-life.

Because I make the bulk of my living as a performing artist and itinerant teacher, I have had many opportunities to interface with children in schools, particularly elementary schools, all over Indiana. One of the songs I often perform is entitled, "Who Are You?" The song is actually an animal guessing game and during its performance I stop periodically for the audience to guess, from the context of the song's clues, which animal I am singing about. It is no real surprise to me that the animal they have the most trouble guessing is Homo sapiens. In fact, afterwards, I have often been confronted with fairly indignant responses from children who contend we are *not* animals at all. A curious notion indeed, but one that adequately sums up our culture's preoccupation with its own self-centered soul. The result is a pervasive ignorance on most of our citizens' parts of many of the animals, plants, and land forms which surround us. And, I might add, any concomitant awareness as to how any of these are connected to our own survival.

All around us, the forests, the croplands, the rivers, lakes, and air are degrading at an exponentially alarming rate, and yet we seem to remain relatively unmoved from our self-destructive path. I am reminded of the oriental proverb that seems so aptly appropriate. In summary, place a frog in a pot. Put the pot on a small fire. The water temperature gradually rises, but the change is so slow the frog cannot detect it. Before too long, the frog is cooked.

Here, in the middle of the hottest summer since 1936, and in a decade that contains five of the driest summers on record, the question remains: How long will it take us to notice that the pot is hot? It certainly looks hot. It feels hot. It measures hot. Still we sit observing. Have we lost the will to free our species from mass suicide or will we wait for word from the experts before we turn inward and begin to make some individual and community-based response?

I believe we can turn our culture's myopic frog-like gaze away from its bigotry toward the natural world and slowly redirect it toward sources which will begin to convey its rebirth. The sources for such a transformation will not be garnered easily but their presence is nearer our noses than anyone might imagine. They are contained within two major dispossessed areas of our communities' lives, each representing an opposite, temporal pole of the other. The first of these aspects is contained within an historic citadel of our culture's shadowy past, repressed from view, prayer, and reflection for such a length of time as to be almost forgotten. The second aspect is contained in that eternal symbol of our communities' hope and future, our children.

I'm sure it is no coincidence that I am composing this essay on the eve of the remembrance of one of the darker chapters in Indiana history. This year marks the 150th year since the hot summer of 1838 when 850 Potawatomi Indians were corralled by state militia near the Twin Lakes in Marshall County and marched out across the hot plains of Indiana, Illinois, and Missouri, to eventually occupy a reservation in Kansas.

The marchers suffered from poor rations and bad water which helped to promote outbreaks of malarial-type fevers that took a heavy toll on their number. More than fifty Potawatomi were buried along the march, many of them young children and tribal elders. This "Trail of Death," as it was christened, stands as an ignoble symbol of our ensuing culture's darkness and deserves a mythic place in all our consciences. It is regrettable to know that its details are often untaught in many Indiana classrooms, and that the drama of its significance is rarely played out in the questioning minds of our children.

It is not easy to face the truth of our own debauchery. Like Columbus and his men's torture, rape, and murder of thousands of Arawak Indians, the Trail of Death stands as a possible signal for engendering a new humility throughout our locality. Before such episodes we all stand, mutually accused and guilty, and from such an awareness we can open our lives to the vast storehouse of wisdom the Native Americans still have in their possession.

In order to effect such a metanoia we need concerted public acts of atonement for past and ongoing misdeeds: lands need to be recommemorated for all of the excommunicated tribes, community forums need to be held with representatives from the tribes present, Native American burial grounds need to be left undisturbed, local histories should be reinvigorated with the truth of these great tribes and their origins, trees need to be planted in communities to honor tribal contributions, and monuments need to be erected to commemorate these great people and their leaders. All these acts and more like them will allow our culture the direct opportunity to attune itself to a great spiritual tradition—a tradition which extends, in some cases, more than 20,000 years preceding our arrival on this continent. If we act bravely, and face the fears we have buried in our pasts, those fears will yield the truths we have kept hidden from our communities for so long a time. These truths can open us to the wisdom these earth-rooted peoples have stewarded in their suffering for so long.

As our communities open themselves through acts that encourage liaisons with tribal ideas and spiritual teachings, they will be gradually awakened to the profound truth which the Native American people realized about their children. Their teachings hold this body of awareness as one of the primary aspects of their culture's longevity, and that is, simply, that like all of the Great Spirit's creations, children are sacred. What is more, from their beginning, they are viewed as important and integral members of the tribe who bring with them a new vision and a new teaching. They are not viewed, as much of this culture views them, as so many empty bodies waiting to be filled with ripe thoughts and plenty of facts, fattened, as it were, for the slaughter of their souls before, to coin a phrase, the mill of particulars. Their children had more of a place than that. Instead, they were seen as signs from the Great Spirit, to be watched and studied, occasionally guided, but generally allowed to discover for themselves the mysteries and significance of this world. In this way they were encouraged toward a great authenticity of spirit.

In reference to the Native Americans, I am reminded of the old adage that we walk through this world standing on our parents' shoulders, and our parents stand on their parents' shoulders, and so on, ad infinitum. Each generation is ascribed a new and higher vantage point (automatically—through birth) which ennobles it to the generation before it.

In Native American cultures, children were encouraged to play and ask questions; they were not continually pushed, prodded, and pulled as so often is the norm today. They were assumed to have a will of their own; it did not need to be constructed for them. They were trusted, in large part, with their own self-direction. In this respect, individual wisdom was seen as something to be nourished, encouraged, and admired. It was a natural acquisition of a person's soul.

My work in Indiana schools has convinced me that the greatest problem our community faces is its own children's lack of self-esteem. In many ways they don't seem to know who they are and where they come from. They are restless and aching for a sense of community. They want adults to recognize them as authentic human beings. They deeply thirst for a sense of belonging. They are lonely, tired, and angry from so much neglect.

A significant way we prevent our children's emotions from transforming us is by channeling them into the world of competitive sports. Here within the vestiges of a simplistic moral order (a win/lose paradigm) we desacralize our children's natural inquisitiveness and we deny them the most important element of a nurturing upbringing—trust. These manic and depressive competitive formulas have disemboweled the basic purposes of public education: the guidance of freethinking individuals who understand the necessity of a cooperative and democratic good. Throughout the classroom, the sports arena, and our society's institutions, the primary driving force of competition at all costs is failing us, because it has insidiously undermined our children's ability to explore cooperative systems that focus on both the independence and the interdependence of the individual. This fixation is nowhere better symbolized than in our religious devotion to sports.

Athletics has become the primary focus and symbol of Indiana schools and communities, leaving socratic models for academic instruction and most of civic and humanitarian thought overlooked and undersupported. In our schools the gymnasium long ago supplanted the library as the major focal point of education. Scholarship, and especially creative authorship and artistry of every kind, is a highly undervalued aspect of our communities' life, and as a result, we have discouraged the thinking skills necessary for our species' survival.

Despite enormous pressure from the shadow-side of our prevailing culture to convert everyone in the educational system to the competitive paradigm, people do resist. It is always heartening to me to realize that children seem to know instinctively that something is remiss about our system's priorities. They know the earth is suffering and something needs to be done about it. They are still close enough (through the integrity of their own birth) to their cooperative natures to understand something is dreadfully wrong with our culture's fanatic competitiveness. When children are entrusted with the responsibility to work with and teach each other through a shared creative experience they begin to relax, let go, and open up to the deep sense of self-esteem all creatures carry within them. For this reason, it is important that children be given significant opportunities to share their creative work and insights within a group which allows them to be vulnerable and aware. As a case in point, I have often worked with children through the creative art of story telling and have encouraged them to compose and tell their own stories in front of peers. In these sessions I have witnessed children rise to the task, full of purpose, and have felt their creative authenticity empower their class-mates toward community.

It is a feeling so electric it is difficult to describe; I only know it is born from giving the children permission to share their feelings in the relative security of creative and cooperative discovery. I have often traveled behind the educational scenes in my role as an artist in Indiana schools and have also heard the teachers whisper these dark truths in their anterooms. They too are tired and discouraged by communities that project their frustrations onto ball-courts and football fields while simultaneously withdrawing their support from the creative development of their own children's minds. Many long for the day when education can become a cooperative endeavor between child, parent, and teacher—promoting the natural thirst for creative synthesis inherent in each child.

We can reinvigorate our educational systems with cooperative ideals by providing our students with a nurturing and supportive environment tuned actively to their creativity and self-expression. Programs can be initiated that begin to redress the one-sided competitive approach which has limited our view of ecological reality for such duration. Scholarships to honor children can be started which encourage creative thinking, designing, drawing, acting, writing, and dancing. Public opportunities to première and display all types of original work by students and citizens should be encouraged. Support for public forums that encourage student participation and representation in government and community issues needs to be forthcoming. In addition, we can reduce the sterility and confinement of the classroom by adding gardens and greenhouses to all our schools, which will enable students to have a first-hand opportunity to see, feel, and study the complex web of their environs. We can enlist the help of children to begin an inventory of each of our communities' surrounding ecosystems. (These inventories can help to provide us with a detailed description of the flora and fauna that still survive. This would enable us to keep a close watch on telltale signs of destructive behaviors which might endanger our ecosystems.) In short (with these ideas and others like them), we can re-empower our children and offer them a place in their own future by making their world more integral and less competitive and threatening, thereby freeing their spirits for the great task at hand. We must move to allow them the opportunity to begin a reconstruction of awareness, an awareness which includes the place where they live and the importance of their lives in it.

Daniel McDonald, Marshall County statesman and author of a *Twentieth Century History of Marshall County*, was an ardent humanist. His interest in the plight of the Potawatomi and their removal from the state of Indiana is in itself inspiring. He was largely responsible for the erection of a commemorative marker to the Potawatomi who lost their lives on the Trail of

Death and their great medicine leader, Menominee. In his history, he recounts
a Potawatomi ceremony enacted shortly before their death march. He describes
the choreography of the ritual like this:

> Many a time old Chief Menominee heard those drowsy cadences from the
> long rows of bronzed warriors at Menominee village at Twin Lakes, now a
> vanished locality. Fainter and fainter grew the melody, until the singers who
> were seated side by side leaned toward each other, drooping closer and closer,
> nearer a reclining position, until gradually one by one pillowed his head on
> his brother's shoulder. Then sleep prevailed so profound that nothing could
> waken it. Yet the constant muffled hum of the pianissimo melody, ''A-e-ah-
> ah!'' to an infinite degree, till the listeners were actually drowsy too!
>
> Then the leader at the head of the row of sleeping warriors roused them
> suddenly with the explosive fortissimo call, ''Ty-ah!'' and again almost si-
> multaneously, by the double fortissimo, ''ugh, Ty-ah!'' Instantly every Indian
> was awake, risen to his feet, all greeting each other noisily and with joy, as
> though they had been parted a long time—many a year!

The title of this ceremony, at least in McDonald's history, is ''Slumber
Song of a Vanished Race.'' I, however, prefer to call it by a directive written
into the last stanza of the song, ''a muffled humming like the droning of the
bees.'' I find the spirit of this line much more to the point of the ceremony.
The Potawatomi, I believe, knew in their wisdom that their influence and
spirit were subsiding, but they also knew that their spirit was intermeshed
with the entire landscape, and to the extent that it survived, they would never
cease to exist. I believe that all who walk deeply on the earth here in northern
Indiana will begin to sense this spirit as they open themselves to each lake,
tree, and animal which resides here. They will feel that continuity between
themselves and their environs which all primal peoples regard as sacred. And
with this feeling in their hearts they will work to protect the earth from their
own human greed.

There is so much in all our lives which we have turned our backs to:
emotions, visions, intuitions, and inner callings of every kind, all suppressed
by our competitive and reductionist approach to living. As we begin the
process of atonement with our past adversary, the Native American, we will
also begin the process of atonement with deeply rejected parts of ourselves.
During this epoch, new fears and emotions will surface and each of us will
need the support which only a strong community can offer us.

In turn, as we reawaken our senses to the importance of our children in the visioning process of our community, we too will feel a new creative empowerment, and work with them for a way out of the pot which has grown so hot. With time, perhaps, we will guide the children at regular intervals out into the field or woods to study and wonder in awe at the intricacy of relationships which all of nature describes. There, perhaps in silence, surrounded by wildflowers and trees, we might first hear the sound. Its hum will float and waver and then suddenly reconnect us to the eternal currents of the universe coursing through our nervous systems. Once again, or so the story goes, we will have returned home.

☙ Mari Evans

ETHOS AND CREATIVITY

The Impulse as Malleable

"BLACK IS my colour," says the poet Lebert Bethune. "Black is my colour . . . The gleaming song of ebony and blood that warms the rivers of the universe—belongs to me." Defines who I am in Indianapolis, shapes the nature of my creativity, influences whether I am creative, and in the final analysis determines how my creativity is received. Whether space is made. And whether I can draw from the atmosphere the nurturing I require to be the most of who I am.

"Black is my colour," says my brother, Bethune. And being Black in Indianapolis is very different from being White in Indianapolis. Each day I am thankful I need no encouragement to be proud of my Africanity, for "proudly Black" is not encouraged. It is, however, tolerated to some extent and people, Black as well as White, I think, attempt rather bravely to coexist with it. What is more acceptable, more comfortable, is a high level of ac-culturation. Definition: "to alter . . . through a process of conditioning."

Don't make waves; don't be unpleasant; and if Truth is unpleasant, then avoid Truth. So I approached this essay with trepidation and much running from face to face to make inquiries, to see if I could nail down, without equivocation, the Truths that are part of my pulse. I often quote myself for somehow I feel (tongue in cheek, of course) that the source is flawless. So I am prone to remind audiences that "in this country we are programmed to disbelieve what we experience," and to suggest that since we are both segment and sum of all that is past it is prudent to be clear about the nature of that past experience as well as the continuing impact it has on how we view society and how we view ourselves.

Many years ago I hosted *The Black Experience*, a television show that aired each Sunday night on a local regional station. The show attempted to answer the question posed by some anonymous poet: "Who will show me myself?" And it is that nostalgic journey over a painful road that I will attempt here. It is a journey I trust will be useful as we search for direction and seriously consider the enormity of the role Ethos plays in the atrophying, or in the nurturing, of the creative spirit.

In a paper prepared to discuss the evolution of African letters, I stated, in regard to the significance of Ethos,

> . . . Concern with the relationship of creativity to encounter is germane. I propose, by way of definition, that creativity is the reaction of the human spirit to the variety of its experiences; a reaction expressed through forms and structures (which may be tonal, verbal, written, visual or physical). . . . Significantly the creative fruit is both determined by, and is as unique as, the intensity of the experiences and the quality of the response. . . . '' In other words, Ethos *is* the environmental laboratory within which creativity, whether positive or negative, roots and is nurtured.

Many years ago I lived in a historic Black community in a section of Indianapolis so close to the heart of town I could walk there in less than fifteen minutes. That community no longer exists. And that is also part of what I need to say here.

Many years ago my father, who had briefly encountered Butler University, in what fashion I never knew, said quietly that he hated Butler. And said it with a passion I could not understand, for I had no notion that he "knew" Butler University.

"Why," I questioned.

"It's racist," he muttered flatly.

"Oh," I said.

And that was that. We had a firm, if subliminal, understanding. I never learned the details, but I supposed it had to do with employment he had sought there. Years later I understood a little better.

My father was hardly verbose; he was succinct, and left little to the imagination. His most serious lapse into profanity was to spit out, "Confound it!" Deeply religious, he was an usher in an African Methodist Episcopal church for fifty years, and for him to say he "hated" anything, even Butler University, was extreme. So I believe his indictment of the university was, in fact, a loose denunciation of the city itself. For it was a place he visited but one in which he could not be persuaded to stay. And early on, when I was very young, I learned why. At least, in part.

While spending part of a summer vacation here I eagerly joined my cousins in the game of saving milk bottle caps for a special free ride day at Riverside Amusement Park. The day came, perfect for an outing, and I suggested saving some of the caps for a later visit only to be informed that there was no other day. This was it. One day a year Black children could come to enjoy the rides. I gave the matter some thought, and, despite the anticipation I had shared, the jeers that I did not expect, made my own childish decision not to go. Langston Hughes speaks for all of us, then, when he says, "There ain't no back to a merry-go-round . . . where's the horse for a kid who's Black?"

So I understand what it means, this knowing that one is "locked out" because of color. Whether it is a public facility such as a museum, or whether it is a public organization, an event, or a school to which a child has been bussed, the subtleties and strategies of "locked out" are easily read and the impact of them as psychologically harmful as they are physically limiting. Those most adept at "locked out" strategies are often those just inside what appears to be the "called-into-being" open door. "Locked out" crushes the spirit and rechannels what could be positive creativity into negative creative acts. "Locked out" is something that can be changed, something that must be changed, because for me, even at that early age, it produced an enormous rage, a rage that should not be dismissed as merely youthful and isolated.

W. E. B. DuBois understood the complexity of living Black in White America, and life for thoughtful, politically informed Black folk who see the society's contradictions clearly is not only complex but filled with the stress of double consciousness. Double consciousness requires keeping one's integrity and sense of his/her Africanity intact while trying to achieve, in the dominant culture—a Herculean task but one to be preferred to the dangers of single consciousness, or "leaving certain of his/her intellectual possessions in pawn" (Fanon, 1967) in order to achieve, or as the price for achieving, in the dominant culture.

Even though I could tell some tales, and sometimes do, about my innate political consciousness at the age of five, one has to experience the acid of psychological locking out that depends on color as the referent—not money, not manners, not clothing, not caste. Color.

When as a young adult I finally settled in Indianapolis, I discovered the marvelous summer nights at Butler's Starlight Musicals Theatre. There were seats way at the top in the back that sold for a dollar and my sons and I could spend an elegant evening under the stars hearing the same music the best seats heard, whenever I had the three dollars plus carfare, of course. The popcorn I made at home, and our thermos contained a fruit drink, sometimes hot to ward off the evening chill. We loved the music, the festive atmosphere, and we could admire the stylish clothing people wore to affairs such as this. We, of course, were appropriately neat and clean, and quite as well-behaved as anyone else in the audience, for that was the way we were, too. But we were still conspicuous, identifiable. Others. And it always seemed to me as if the value of the seats adjacent to ours fell a bit when we sat down. But we liked our seats. They were not only closer to the stars, they were close to the exits, and when the performance was over we could hurry out and escape the slow-moving crowd.

We were also regulars at the symphony. For the free concerts, that is. I remember feeling quite superior about attending the free concerts, as a matter of fact. That, I contended, set the real music lover apart from those who merely attended opening and subscription concerts because it was the thing to do, the place to be seen. We, I would whisper to the boys, in the words of a Gwendolyn Brooks poem, "are the real thing. . . . " We come because of the music since there certainly is no panache about being "seen" at a free concert.

Those were very special Sundays. We would hurry home from church, feel very provident and orderly over the casserole succulent and waiting in the oven, then rush to the corner to stand in whatever the weather, to wait for the bus to town. Since the symphony encompasses the entire winter season, it was often blustery, and freezing winds would whip around the three of us standing close together for warmth. But we were bundled well, and we stamped our feet constantly to keep the blood circulating.

There was, for me at least, a moment of absolute ecstasy when, wraps undone and deposited in a nearby empty seat, we could settle down in the midst of the Murat's faded red velvet and flaked gilt and escape into the cacophony of the orchestra's tuning. We preferred front row first balcony seats and tried to arrive early enough to insure that we had them.

There was one indelible moment when a tall Korean guest conductor, having distinguished himself during the first part of the scheduled program, swept through the velvet curtain at our left clad in a long black opera cape, and found a seat close by. We were enthralled.

Indianapolis, I tell friends in other places, is a city where the preservation of Euro-American cultural traditions and the enhancement of those traditions has been consistent. Not only consistent but increasingly an economic factor too significant to be ignored or dismissed. The arts are not only encouraged but subsidized. The City of Indianapolis has on occasion subsidized the arts to the extent that federal money earmarked for the relief of concerns affecting the disadvantaged was, during one administration, diverted to the Ballet Theatre. From a Black perspective this was unconscionable and could not be rationalized away.

Mario Cuomo, governor of New York, while addressing the 1984 Democratic Convention, said in his now-historic speech: "This nation is more a *Tale of Two Cities* than it is a shining city on a hill." Cuomo was replying to statements of then-President Reagan whose "supply side" or "trickle down" theories had already set a new pace for the national government's response to the country's special and economic problems. Cuomo admitted that the country is "a shining city for those lucky enough to live in its good neighborhoods. But for the people who are excluded, locked out, all they can do is stare from a distance at that city's glimmering towers. It's an old story," he said, "as old as our history."

And so it is with Indianapolis. Looking back over almost four decades, everything has changed and nothing has changed. This, too, is a tale of two cities. For me, and close to 150,000 other persons of African descent living in this city, it has been—a Black experience.

Memory is capricious, eclectic. Certain names, captured moments, Today's recall of Yesterday's incredible tenderness, its secret pain. Today's instant replay: Yesterday on parade, still fresh in the heart. A waft of perfume or the lingering odor of rage now decayed.

Late Sunday afternoons, the Mme. Walker tearoom stylishly packed, crisp gloves, the soft silks gleaming. The western sky awash with red-orange, vivid to pastel, stroked with delicate purples, sunset viewed with awe from a fourth floor project window.

Lockefield. Ah, yes. Lockefield . . .

For the span of my memory this has been a city of opposing wills, two faces firmly set toward different directions—one covertly determined to maintain the status quo, to continually block any access to power, or to parity; one, advocating an active morality and its right to inclusion as an equal person rather than a colonized one. This has been a city of perpetual confrontation, however cloaked, between the powerless and those who influence, control, and engineer the city's movement in its inexorable and often ruthless march toward "greatness," a word for which my definition will hardly suffice.

It is an American story, the leitmotif of a nation whose contradictions are all the more searing here, in a prospering highly visible "all-American City," than elsewhere.

In the beginning, in most of the Black enclaves throughout Indianapolis and even on "The Avenue" itself, there were dreams to go around, and the belief that attainment logically followed determined effort was contagious. Nearly everyone had plans, destinations, "goals," whether articulated or merely smoldering in some recess of the collective mind. Black folk were firmly convinced that with hard work and a "good" disposition the future was theirs for the taking. The group worked every bit as hard as it played, fed on its understanding of unlimited possibility, and gave off an enormous energy.

The Indiana Avenue area was what I knew best. At one time it stretched in a sprawling, random way (and always "approximately") from 16th and Illinois Street to the Avenue's matrix, to Senate Avenue, to Michigan, to Fall Creek, to Tenth and so on. It included the smart new Flanner House homes, erected through sweat equity contracts, and the proud new Fall Creek YMCA. "The Avenue" began and ended in town, and "town" always seemed to be one's destination whenever one ventured outside the brotherhood, the sisterhood of the community; one only worked elsewhere.

Once while employed as a typist I was invited to my employer's home for dinner. Although I cannot remember what she served, I remember vividly how difficult it was to get there, how long my sons and I stood on street corners transferring from bus to meandering bus, and I remember wondering what her neighbors thought about her iconoclastic socializing. It was not, I understood, a usual gesture for that particular community. She lived, if I remember correctly, on Haverford near Kessler. At that time the only persons of color who frequented the area were Black domestics and yard men.

Indianapolis was not the city then that it is now. Downtown was simply "downtown." No malls, no glitz, no glitter. The outlying areas, the "bedroom communities," while connoting all that the phrase implies, were merely places that were geographically difficult and time consuming to reach by public transportation. Broad Ripple I knew by name only. Meridian Hills had a mystic quality, a sort of "golden" aura. They were places White folk of some substance lived and striving Black folks of little substance either worked or were invited by liberal Whites to visit. I rarely lost my sense of two cities.

Many Black folk thought of Indianapolis as urban, "up South." It was better than being "down South," but it retained many of the negative propositions of the deep South, and was not yet as enlightened or "progressive" as its West or East Coast counterparts. Conservatism and racism were alive and compatible.

To our discredit there is, even today, an amazing retention of that early sensibility. It is expressed, however, with much more class, much more elan, and many Black folk are so enthralled by the smiles they do not read the eyes nor understand psychological "locking out."

Then, if one had ambitions one knew that ultimately the only way to realize them fully would be to leave the comfort and the encouragement of one's neighborhood for some far city more responsive to one's skills.

The neighborhood was sustaining. Children were protected and insulated by classrooms manned by Black teachers who cared passionately about their charges' future, who saw promise in them, loved them, chastised them promptly, and encouraged them to be more than even they envisioned. School was not a place where teachers and staff feared Black students, not a war zone nor a place of controlled pain and anguish that manifested itself in student indifference and rebellion. Those schools were places where Black children understood that above all else they were loved, and being cared for with love.

Since busing, one can make no such blanket statement about the dynamics of education for Black children in the Indianapolis and township schools.

In the communities of which I was a part there were the athletes, legendary, soon-to-be national figures remembered for their high school prowess and their alma mater no matter which professional team they might sign with or star for later. Today's athletes train, perform, and disappear into colleges across the nation. They are not hugged to the collective bosom; there is no "collective bosom," there is no "we."

When the city was ready to phase in its plans to appropriate the area for the economic convenience and pleasure of its dominant White population, bulldozers cut swaths through first one and then another of the Black com-

munities. Small houses that stood in the way of such progress brought minuscule ''market value'' amounts to their protesting owners, amounts that in
no way reflected the years of hard labor, of ''scrimping'' and ''scraping,''
and love, that had been invested. Homes crumbled as insignificant Black
home owners, many already elderly, watched powerlessly, their protests lost
in the steel-on-steel of advancing heavy machinery. They had become that
era's ''new poor'' through no fault of their own and with the help of the city's
machinations many would soon see their names added to the welfare rolls.

Black people did not want the expressway to come through their neighborhoods, but it did, displacing them, their way of life, their cohesiveness,
their sense of themselves as persons who have value, who matter.

If men and women cannot defend their land, their homes, their life's work,
their accomplishments, against a determined government of people unlike
themselves, they understand themselves only too clearly as ''non people,''
and they understand that they are perceived as ''non people'' in the minds
of their own government. Is geography, whether in North America or South
Africa, a significant qualifier when bulldozers raze the homes of the poor,
the Black, the powerless?

Black people did not want the schools in their neighborhoods emptied of
their children and closed. Busing? For some, the answer was yes; for many
more, the answer has always been ''no!'' But for all, the only acceptable
solution would have been to apply the disruption of busing across the board
to all children, not primarily and mainly to Black children. Across the board
dislocation did not happen. No Decatur Central children are bused into my
neighborhood, for the school in my neighborhood is closed.

When the realization set in that the Black community was expendable,
that our homes, schools, churches, businesses, playgrounds were expendable—that we, in fact, were expendable—something changed. Something
indefinable that ate away at the core of our togetherness, clawed away some
of the dreams, and consumed many of those less able to survive.

Chaos and anger and hostility followed. We began, gradually, to hear
more and more about ''Black on Black crime'' as the powerless began to
fight among themselves, for the real opponent was too well entrenched, his
control seemed almost absolute, and his ''weaponry'' much too sophisticated,
too state-of-the-art for the community to successfully engage. But oh, they

did try. I found clippings and photographs, articles about confrontations, and snapshots of press conferences. And nothing has changed but the language. The community did try. But the dispersal, the fragmentation, the wanton obliteration left their legacy. It was a legacy of broken spirit, and it brought with it an insidious sense of hopelessness that would subliminally infect all levels of the Black community for several decades. This was hopelessness born of a new, more biting realization of Black powerlessness. It defined in ways much more powerful than words our involuntary subordinance to a white city structure whose aims, plans, and desires were significantly different from our own, and it said our absolute vulnerability to that structure's caprice. Nevertheless, the Black community's leaders continued to strive and the common folk still struggled to overcome in the face of a disdainful system.

Somehow the line from the civil rights classic "We Shall Overcome," with its wistful "someday" as a sardonic tag, has always seemed extraordinarily cynical when sung in the midst of the structured dismemberment of a racial group. It is difficult to explain "destruction" in the midst of construction and plenty, or to "prove" a destroyed environment in the midst of modern renovation, elegance, and urban beauty that is almost sylvan in its perfection. Difficult to find the anger to rail at such beauty, except that the destruction, the "locking out," has also been psychological—and has left such apathy in its wake. The accommodations, the compromises have taken their toll.

One would have to have known the people, walked the streets. To understand the enormity of what transpired, one would have to have been there, somewhere in the beginning, during that time when hope boogalooed, time-stepped, and literally "ran wild" down the Avenue and throughout the flurry of neighborhoods that comprised the city's Black community.

The planned obsolescence of a thriving Black community near the heart of the city was eventually successful and resulted in the demolition of schools, private homes, churches, small Black businesses, private social facilities, public recreation areas, and most importantly the general destruction of a sense of community and a way of life that was in fact the matrix for many of today's Black "gentry." We are talking, still, of Ethos and how powerfully it impacts the spirit, for none of this could have happened without the blessing and the contrivance of the official city government:

1976

> I can assure you . . . I feel that the area occupied by the Lockefield Garden
> Apartments is critical to the expansion . . . we . . . feel that the Lockefield
> area should be demolished and made available . . . as well as . . . (Excerpted
> from a local administrator's letter to the Indianapolis Department of Metro-
> politan Development, November 3, 1976)

1988

LOCKEFIELD GARDENS
DOWNTOWN LIVING AT ITS BEST

> A National Historic Landmark, built in 1936, Lockefield Gardens once again
> brings the tradition of urban living to life. Experience the exciting renaissance
> of downtown Indianapolis as a resident of this distinctive new apartment com-
> munity. Lockefield Gardens—where the past embraces the future for the way
> you live today. (Excerpted from descriptive/promo for the newly designed and
> erected as well as renovated Lockefield Gardens, September, 1988)

The community is gone. Razed. Bulldozed. Its striving, hopeful population scattered to the fringes of nowhere. Removed in the name of progress,
to make room for the new population waiting, figuratively, on the drafting
board. A new area, smart, new people—very few of whom look anything
like those dispossessed.

It was the replacement, the substitution of one kind of person for another
just as desirous of a good life, that left a bitterness, created a deep psychological rift—a lasting hurt beneath the trauma, from which Indianapolis will
be slow to recover. Particularly since the wound has only been exacerbated,
not healed by the city's subsequent insensitivity to many other issues of
African-American concern.

There are still smiles, there are still handshakes, speeches about progress
and revitalization made by a few Black and many White entrepreneurs from
both the private and public sectors. Black and White heads nod sagely, and
Blacks scurry for grants and pull and scrape in a more sophisticated manner
than their forefathers, to curry favor, to "get along," and to "get over." But
no one is fooled. Everything takes place over the ever-present battered body

of the victim. The fresh new buildings, the careful designer-tech landscaping are constant and bitter reminders of Black powerlessness. And White power.

All this is Ethos. And it is within this frame that the Black creative spirit comes to some resolute if battered fruition. Small wonder that our art is pulsed by political nuances. The real wonder is that in the hands, nationally, of our finest practitioners Black artistry remains aesthetically competitive enough to capture, over the years, Pulitzers in poetry, literature, and theatre.

There is, however, anger and a residual bitterness that is very much alive in the Black community. It is anger nurtured by the continuing history of police violence against the city's Black residents. Although paralleled by police actions, shootings and brutality in other cities, it is certainly no more palatable. Indianapolis has a record of brutality and unconscionable mayhem that is historical, one that cannot be dismissed. Police racism is not accidental, nor is it merely the capricious acts of a few "bad apples." But, if it *is* capricious, then the horror escalates, for not once in the last twenty years has any policeman been convicted of the unjustified killing of a Black person. Each Black death has been steadfastedly justified, endorsed, and unqualifiedly supported by the hierarchy of city and police officials who have consistently found the officers involved blameless.

The most recent justification by the Indianapolis Police Department is that of the Michael Taylor death. Michael Taylor, a sixteen-year-old Black, clad only in a tank top, shorts, sneakers, and socks, allegedly shot himself in the temple while seated in the back of a police car, his wrists firmly handcuffed behind him. The case has been officially closed. This finding was supported by the Black community's independent investigation that had somehow been turned over to a retired Indianapolis deputy chief of police. After a lifetime of good and faithful service in the department, and after having carefully risen to such unheard-of heights, it hardly mattered that he was Black. Many citizens, Black and White, who still insist on justice in the Michael Taylor death understand all too well that it is the city's hierarchy, the powers behind the thrones, that they fight, not merely the police department.

Obviously the experience of Indianapolis' Black citizens with the city's police department is searing, brutal, and deadly in too many instances. The indelible message, one that cannot be misconstrued, is that Black life is expendable; Black people do not count as "people."

Again we raise the issue of Ethos and its impact on the human mind and spirit when the climate is one of trauma and almost unmitigated stress. For many of the city's Black citizens this is merely part of what living in Indianapolis is all about.

Of course there are other ways Black folk experience Indianapolis and I, too, as integral with the group, experience those with considerable pleasure.

I enjoy fine restaurants, I frequent the museums. A tennis hacker since I was twelve, I am a regular at the pro and exhibition matches. I am a sports buff, so Olympic trials, cross-country skiing, Pan Am Games, here I come. And I blessed Indianapolis when it named the Velodrome after Major Taylor without my assistance; confessing, now publicly, that if it had not been for the city I might never have known about Major Taylor. I've enjoyed the marvelous New Zoo, looked forward to the Circle City Classic at the domed stadium, and am sorry I missed the Colts game with the Bears.

As we've said, this is a lovely city, and with considerable ambivalence I admit: it engages one aesthetically in the most delightful way. And it is true—a lot has changed in Indianapolis over the last four decades. Certainly the city has prospered if a changing skyline is synonymous with prosperity.

It is also true that a significant segment of the Black community has done well. There is a coterie of wealthy Black residents, and, scattered throughout the city, a community of affluent young Blacks. Upwardly mobile, some have been attracted to the city because of its new cosmopolitan reputation; some have chosen to settle here because of the availability of corporate slots for bright young Black folk convinced both of their own skill at "gamesmanship" and their capacity to "hang." While this is also what living in Indianapolis means, it is such a minuscule part that I mention it merely to keep the record straight. Locked out is not total; it merely prevails.

Indianapolis is truly dichotomous, a city in which contradictions are the norm. It is easy to be deluded here, especially when one *prefers* delusion to clarity. It may be that, due to our high visibility, Black musicians seem to abound. This is, however only partially true and then of certain areas/places—not across the board. Indeed, a common complaint among many members of the Black music community in Indianapolis is that although appropriately skilled and available, they are, with few exceptions, discriminated against by local entrepreneurs or contractors who hire for the lucrative but—more importantly—emotionally gratifying sidemen jobs that occur when major artists perform in the Indianapolis area: Even when the artists happen to be African

American the backup musicians hired will invariably be White. Moreover, with a few exceptions, African American musicians are almost frozen out of the more prestigious and better paying engagements despite the reservoir of excellent Black talent.

The usual response to the charge of economic racism in music in Indianapolis is the institutionalized "We can't find a competent one." Because of its inaccuracy the allegation is insulting and demeaning to the city's Black musicians, whose rebuttal invariably has been, "You don't *want* a competent one; you don't want any."

Incredibly, and against the logic of the dollar, the manager of an elegant hotel lounge admitted that in his *hope* to attract more White customers he was changing the room's orientation from jazz to pop or country. His stated intent was to eliminate the burgeoning African American audience, however chic and well behaved, that had over the past months filled the room past capacity.

The litany of superior Black talent lost to Indianapolis because no opportunity to grow creatively and to prosper economically existed here reads like a page from some international *Who's Who*: Curry, Baker, J. J. Johnson, Ridley, Spaulding, Webster, et al. The problem for African Americans has always been political. It has never been a problem of talent, or a problem of competency as is often claimed. The problem has always been where to take an enormous potential or a superior talent. If there are not areas into which the artist can expand, and if the Ethos is hostile and nonreceptive, how long will he or she push the creative urge to its periphery? Major Black talents decay and atrophy in Indianapolis because there is nowhere for them to "go"; no impetus toward an escalating creative explosion because there has been no forum, no platform, no arena in which to develop. There is a compulsion to grow that every creative artist feels if his spirit, nurtured by his reality, has any reason at all to sense for itself some future fulfillment. It has been about politics in Indianapolis; not about art, not about creativity. Other than Kevin Pugh, how many of Indianapolis' Black youth have come through the Indianapolis Ballet Theatre during the span of its existence? Is it because we can't dance?

Black creative artists are part of the fringe element the Reverend Jackson talks about when he speaks of "those locked out" of society's normal channels, society's usual, often subsidized, always-encouraged routes to maximization. It has been about politics, it has never been about talent.

We may be able to live with the fact that young Black adults have to leave Indiana to find the recognition, the inclusion, and the opportunity to grow their talent deserves. Although this is also true of many young Whites, I would argue that the similarity ends there. For, when Whites leave, whatever the reason, they know they have not been rejected or "locked out" because their skin is white. But can we live with the unconscionable waste of creative potential that is caused by Indiana's failure to find important the death of that potential in its Black citizens?

At a recent gathering I was struck by the sincerity of one speaker who encouraged a "system of freedom of expression." Struck, because the artistic community that I am on occasion invited to join seems to regard art and politics as separate and conflicting entities, all experience to the contrary. In such a climate, of course, creative expression is not freely extended to political viewpoints that are at variance to what is considered the norm. In fact a rather firm line is drawn, a line that can become far from subtle if occasion demands. My experience has shown that often even discourse becomes a matter of broken field running for all involved—Black/White liberals, Black/White conservatives. And there I sit—symbolic of all the social ills that creativity in Indiana is expected to transcend. There I sit.

What we find is that racism, in this up-South city at the end of the twentieth century, is like a steel strand encased in nylon then covered in some luxurious fabric. The intent is to avoid, if possible, blatant offenses, to soothe, mollify, if necessary dissemble—while racism, the steel strand, still effectively does the job.

All this is Ethos. We have been examining an Ethos that, in matters that are substantive, is limiting and restrictive. And Ethos is a shaping element, maybe the most influential of all the factors that impact on the ultimate empowering of, or destruction of, the Black creative spirit in Indiana, or elsewhere.

The creative urge to be, or to do, springs as directly from our Ethos as day and night from the earth's turnings. Impetus requires a matrix. Therefore, if Ethos is our shaping matrix, and if the arts community is concerned with exploring Indiana as Ethos, and if being Black in Indiana (or more specifically,

Indianapolis) is measurably different from being White, then a different Black response to the challenge of, or lack of challenge from, the Ethos may well be expected.

A difference in focus and concern is a very natural requisite to what are contrived and unnatural situations. It is not so simple as whether one will or will not elect to respond to the circumstances of Ethos. Challenge elicits response and the response may just as easily be negative as positive.

In other words, the creative urge is called forth by what one experiences within one's Ethos. The creative spirit will respond fully and positively if the forum exists, if possibility stands plainly in view; this is the time when challenge has been received and understood.

If the creative urge, responding to what for the Black community is the ongoing stress and trauma of Ethos, is not empowered or enabled to produce positively because that possibility has not been disclosed, the creative fruit may either atrophy unexpressed, or it may find expression in ways that are negative and socially destructive. The first of these two options represents a tremendous human and cultural loss to society, the latter a tremendous waste of tax dollars in erecting and maintaining bases of short-range semi-control. And, in my experience, Indianapolis has issued very few clear creative challenges to its Black residents.

Moreover, if there is validity in my definition of creativity one can find some rationale for the exodus of Black talent from Indiana and the subsequent explosion of world-class creativity by Black Indiana natives in more hospitable places around the globe.

There are a few exceptions—musicians, writers, artists who retain Indiana as their base but look outside the state for fulfillment: notably, the late Wes Montgomery who deliberately subordinated his career to other priorities; Dr. David N. Baker, Chairman of the Jazz Department and distinguished Professor of Music on Indiana University's, Bloomington campus. A major composer, director, performer, and a figure of international renown, his creative genius receives greater exposure on the world's stage than in Indiana. Certainly none of his major works have been performed by the Indianapolis Symphony. Finally, and most recently, the exit of William Henry Curry from Indianapolis to a rural retreat. In a state known more for its open real estate market than for its open attitude toward the arts, Curry's experience as associate conductor of the Indianapolis Symphony Orchestra rarely allowed him to demonstrate that he is considered by many of the national classical hierarchy the premier young conductor in the country. Curry, at thirty-three, now joins the ranks of Black expatriates whose enormous prestige in their fields quite paradoxically serves to enhance Indiana's out-of-state image. No matter how the state's arts communities, and arbiters, may choose to ignore the significance of this explosion of Black talent that occurs outside Indiana's borders, the ironic dimensions of the pattern are not lost on most observers.

To the man in the street it appears that the arts in Indianapolis are supported by the city's elite. Top corporations, firms, businesses, and prestigious and wealthy individuals seem to give both their money and their time to participate in the cultural life of the city. And are not these same individuals, corporations, firms, and businesses—the city's movers and shakers—the back room designers of city policy? In ways that often appear inexplicable, blacks are tacitly excluded from the channels that access power.

Maybe the arts community, which is central to the city's effective development and necessary for its continued growth, can do something to rectify what appears to be tacit but in-place policy, not merely a capricious practice. If it decides it can or will, and a clear, cold intellectual decision is called for, then it will need to examine its own heart. It is there that change, the railing against its own hypocrisy, must begin. I know. It is about politics.

Engaged in the process of summation, at one conference, a participant admonished, ''Don't bring me your ills'' a statement reflective of Indiana's rather classic mindset. ''Ills,'' however, are an integral part o583f the larger picture, part of Ethos, part of Indiana, and they must also become a concern of the arts before giant steps can be taken to maximize the uses of culture in order to enhance the quality of life for all of Indiana's citizens.

We began this essay with the loose premise that although many things do change in Indianapolis, many significant others, including the city's obvious disdain for its Black citizens, remain very much the same:

City Requests "Delisting" of Avenue
from Historical Register

''The last straw.'' That's what a number of the city's Black leaders are calling the city's latest episode in a long list of developments which have led to the downfall of Indiana Avenue. . . . Removal from the Register (of Historic Places) would leave nine buildings on the Avenue vulnerable to the City's wrecking ball. . . . '' (*Indianapolis Recorder*, October 29, 1988)

* * *

Black is my colour . . .
The force that swarms the sky
At the apogee of a strange night
Engulfing the white moon
Belongs to me.

—Lebert Bethune

🐁 Teresa Ghilarducci

HOOSIER WOMEN IN A MALE ECONOMY

I ASSURED them at my job interview that I wanted to move from Berkeley, California, to a midwestern industrial city. What labor economist wouldn't? In fact, the first time I had heard of South Bend was a reference to the South Bend Lathe Company, one of the most famous modern worker-owned firms. Only later did I link the city with the University of Notre Dame, my employer. Displaced workers and economic dislocation were my research areas and I wanted to be where the action was. I wasn't disappointed. In 1983, I found a rust bowl region that replaced its high-paying manufacturing jobs with low-paying service and retail jobs. But, by 1984, I discovered another side of the economy.

That year the South Bend School secretaries linked up with the Teamsters and petitioned the School Board for a union election. Although, in years past, the board had granted the janitors and groundskeepers union elections, it refused the secretaries' request. The Teamsters union responded with what turned out to be a savvy strategic and consciousness-raising move. They sued the School Board for sex discrimination for denying the female-dominated union what the board had given male unions. Their lawsuit triggered the formation of a coalition between labor unions and local women's groups. Union and labor issues often bypass the South Bend female economy. Here, women are union members almost by accident, when they work in male-dominated jobs. Women work primarily in nonunion jobs, or in the non-paid home economy, and are wives, sisters, and daughters of male union members. The Teamster lawsuit—it eventually yielded a union-won election—transformed the labor union issue into a women's issue and helped transform my own research and sensibilities in the process.

The secretaries organizing excited the community and I, as a labor economist, was bombarded with requests from community women for data on the status of working women in South Bend. These women were from churches, poverty agencies and shelters, peace groups, community service agencies, and the local chapter of the National Organization of Women (formed in the 1970s to push for ratification of the Equal Rights Amendment). This group of women, along with some men from the local labor unions, organized the Working Women's Coalition. I became a member and the designated statistician. They wanted answers to questions about the female side of the economy that no business, union, or public official had ever asked before. What do women earn in South Bend and in Indiana? How many work? How many are poor? What happens to women when men are economically displaced? What happens to women when they don't have access to men's income? Who benefits from sex discrimination? This "feminized" focus on the South Bend economy also drew attention to children and raised another question—how does South Bend (and Indiana) treat its children?

These questions had no answers because, in the business community's and government's discussions, 45% of Indiana's full time workers weren't consulted, weren't regarded, and didn't have a face in government statistics. Planners have a limited range of vision. They focus on men's jobs and the future of male earners, attempting to lure steel mills and other manufacturing plants, creating low tax enterprise zones, and providing job retraining. Women working in low paying jobs in the highly profitable retail trade and service sectors have experienced hardship and family dislocation, but these developments are applauded, not scrutinized. Because women's concerns are not seen, a vital part of the economy is ignored and the massive dislocation of the non-market home economy goes unnoticed.

Life here (and throughout the U.S. in varying degrees) is hard up against a dissonance between reality and beliefs about the role of women in society. Fewer than 20% of Indiana's households are families where dad works to support a nonworking mom and kids. However, schools, the work place, the church, and the cultural milieu encourage a fantasy suburban, 1950s-like vision that what kids do during the day is a private matter. We act as if mom is waiting after school with moral instruction and milk and cookies. More likely (63% of mothers work), mom is in a dead-end low-paying job. Though I am a labor economist I feel like an archeologist or psychiatrist, uncovering the truths that have always been present. Uncovering statistics about women workers gives women workers an identity and a presence.

An unintended consequence of my "statistical uncovering" was the uncovering of my own childhood. I came to understand my experiences in Roseville, California, in the context of a broader social phenomenon. By examining Indiana I discovered that the way a society treats its women governs the way it treats its children's education and welfare. My childhood was split in two. In the first half I lived in an intact, "traditional" family; in the second half I lived with my mother and brother and became part of what is now called the "feminization of poverty." My mother worked full time, but earned poverty wages. She/we experienced the economic consequences of sexism. Thirteen years ago I began to study the same phenomenon as an adult.

I circulated some statistics on the economic consequences of sexism. They showed that the wage gap here was greater than in the nation as a whole. For every dollar earned by a white male worker in 1970, his female counterpart received 69 cents. But if that woman worked in St. Joseph County, she received only 54 cents. This ratio has remained virtually the same since the end of World War II. Also, since World War II Hoosier women have participated in the labor force at rates higher than the U.S. average. So more Hoosier women work, and they are paid less.

I was surprised at the reaction these statistics provoked in the community. Women became angry and men defensive; a battle was forming that pitched women workers against male workers. I became profoundly aware of this false fight when I was in a television studio waiting to be interviewed. A young male technician snickered nervously, "Don't be too hard on us guys." He seemed half guilty and half threatened by the mere exposure of women's problems in the economy and by a women's economy. What he didn't see, and what the Working Women's Coalition hadn't emphasized, is that, ironically, male workers don't benefit from sexism in the long run. On one level most people understand that: women certainly don't see men improving their status when sex discrimination persists.

A recent trend helps illustrate this point. The narrowing of the U.S. sex-pay gap has recently been news. Are women "winning" against men? Sadly, no. The gap narrowed because men's real pay has fallen by 9.5%, while women's real earning increased by only 3.2%.

Because, in South Bend, women filled approximately 85% of the new jobs in the last fifteen years (a similar trend is predicted for the U. S.) one can't understand the labor market without understanding institutionalized sexism—a social construct in which subjective and objective expectations, opportunities, and resources are determined largely by one's sex.

One form of sexism is unequal pay for equal work. It's technically illegal, but in the U.S. and in Indiana in hundreds of occupations women are paid less than men. (In South Bend, women in only three occupations earn more than men, and by just a few percentage points—auto mechanics, nurses, and telephone operators.)

National studies indicate that a woman will earn 20% less than a man even if she has the same work experience, number of children, job, level of education, and union status, and lives in the same area. My mother had some college education but she, like most women, was making less than male high school dropouts. Most employers don't pay men more than women for the same job because of personal feelings of malice or sexism. Many wage rates in nonunionized settings are established in individual bargaining sessions with employers. In 1984, recruiters for new MBA's said they preferred to interview women because they could comfortably offer them $10,000 less than they would a man. A woman's bargaining position is weaker and when salary is set by individual bargaining power women are paid less. Since starting salaries and merit pay are also based on real and perceived bargaining power, women also fall behind throughout their working lives. They may have the same occupation, but fine distinctions made between job titles provide a way to pay less to women with nearly identical jobs. Yet, in the case I just cited, a woman's weaker bargaining position resulted in an unemployed male MBA. The lowest paid worker gets the job.

Another form of sexism is reflected in the fact that occupations are segregated by sex and "women's jobs" pay less than male-dominated jobs. The mere presence of females in a particular job lowers pay. In 1984, the earnings of female college graduates would decline by 4.2% for every ten percent increase in the proportion of females in their occupation. The Working Women's Coalition in South Bend discovered that in County and City employment women were concentrated in jobs paying almost 20% less than male-dominated jobs. In seventeen job categories, in the City of South Bend, only 4 had men and women employed in them.

The combination of two facts—women are filling four out of five new jobs created, and jobs designated as "women's jobs" pay less—explains why the proportion of middle-income jobs is diminishing. Retail, service and finance and insurance jobs are paying less than $20,000 per year because women are filling those jobs, not because the employers can't afford to pay more. Shopping malls, banks, insurance companies, and health-related industries are among the most profitable in the nation.

Eliminating sex discrimination might reverse the growth of low-paying jobs; women's jobs would pay more and women would be paid the same as men in the same job. This might inhibit the growth of executive salaries and the profits of the very highest income class—beneficiaries of sexism—but the number of middle-income jobs would not have to diminish.

Moreover, the devaluation of women's jobs distorts social and human assessment of what is dear and what is cheap. In Indiana, parking lot attendants are paid more than child care workers. The market, the single-most important arbiter of relative value in our society, devalues what we value most.

Laws requiring that comparable jobs be paid comparably would solve these problems and more. Employers couldn't threaten men with the prospect of hiring women and women's work would not be devalued. This would mean child care, nursing, and elementary school teaching would become more valued professions.

The powerful influence gender roles have on market outcomes diffuses the idea that people freely choose their own oppression and that government can't do anything about inequality. Institutional sexism in the form of wage and occupational discrimination is not a battle of the sexes; it is one element in the conflict between employers and workers, because any exploitable group in the labor force threatens the status of all workers in an economy. Professor Ruth Needleman of Indiana University Northwest has documented how white male Indiana steelworkers sought to promote the status of blacks because the steel companies used blacks to break strikes and undermine the steelworkers' unions. An even older generation of Hoosier workers understood how another social construct worked against them. Employers tried to use xenophobia to exaggerate differences between the working-class immigrants. The Poles, Irish, Italians, Catholics, and Jews overcame the efforts to divide them and formed strong unions.

Women workers are the new immigrants, the new exploitable group. And, in a manner similar to racism or xenophobia, sexism fosters the belief that women have different work motivations than men. Just as xenophobia encouraged the belief that immigrants had allegiances to other nations and were not so committed as workers as the native-born, sexism would have us believe women are less able to work in many jobs because of their sex. Similarly, blacks, and Eastern and Southern European immigrants, were deemed to have low intelligence because of their race and ethnicity. Social constructs that divide workers and undermine some create downward pressure on the status of all workers.

Only by understanding how institutional sexism obscures what women and men have in common can we understand why—when male workers are harmed by sexism—people still believe that women's gains come only at the expense of men. An old but still poignant lesson from the feminist movement explains the paradox that, although female and male workers are harmed by sexism, both groups promote it. As long as women are separated from men and what is feminine and masculine remains germane, the mutual harm will continue unnoticed and women will strike out at the wrong target. Sex, what is male and female, is biological. Gender, what is feminine and masculine, is manufactured by society. When what is "feminine" and "masculine" are foremost, then gender is used to allocate tasks and responsibilities. However, social rules and customs that rely on gender can be inefficient. Instead of distributing tasks by people's individual talents, abilities, and interests, our society assigns tasks at birth. Ever wonder why the first thing asked about a child is whether it's a boy or girl? It's not insignificant; it's a job assignment. Sex is a convenient organizing tool in a complex world. Yet, the best person for a particular job may never be in a position to be hired as long as men and women are artificially divided.

Sex segregation is well underway by elementary school. In South Bend, girls' test scores decline as they get older and fall behind boys' at high school level. In South Bend, girls are equally represented in middle-level math courses, but a disproportionate number of boys are in advanced and remedial math courses—special care is taken with male math achievement. In vocational programs, students enroll in programs identified with sex roles. Girls dominate the clerical and food service programs.

Whenever I refer to a student's dissertation I am directing, or the activities of one of my students, or refer to someone as my graduate assistant, many people, not just Hoosiers, unfailingly assume my student or assistant is a woman, although most of the time I am talking about men. Gender roles are so entrenched that even though I teach at Notre Dame (where only 28% of the students are female) the idea that I have authority over a male is discounted.

Strict gender roles limit women's achievement in the worlds of commerce and ideas and men's achievement in the worlds of emotion and children. Men's assigned roles are first as breadwinners and second as fathers. Men are more likely to be separated by market work from their children. When a divorce occurs men are more likely to be separated from their children. Eighty percent of children with divorced parents live with their mothers. A human tragedy, indeed. Women who have sole custody of their children, however, are often faced with economic tragedy.

Institutionalized sexism causes women and children's economic status to decline after a divorce. It has been said that most women are one man away from poverty, and that axiom certainly holds true in Indiana. Support for women and children who don't have access to male incomes is abysmally low—the median monthly welfare payment in Indiana is under $230 per month. Ohio and Illinois pay nearly $300 per month. Indiana ranks 30th among states in per capita income, but we are 38th in welfare expenditure, Guam pays higher benefits than Indiana.

Indiana's attention to children's education is also low, relative to the nation's and our state's ability to pay. We rank 30th in income, but we rank 34th in elementary school expenditures and 35th in expenditures for higher education. In the U.S. almost 1 out of 4 three- and four-year-olds is in a pre-school program; in Indiana the ratio is less than 1 in 8.

My research into women and children in Indiana made me realize how I benefited from growing up in California. In the pattern typical of kids from divorced families, my brother and I lived primarily on my mother's low earnings. The "E.O.P." financed my way to the University of California. Only during my first day on campus, at the E.O.P. orientation (where the majority of the students were black), did I learn E.O.P. meant Equal Opportunity Program. Even though I was different from these students—I was white and both my mother's parents and grandparents and my father graduated from college—I still needed state aid and Medicaid to go to the public university. And since California valued public education I went to one of the best universities in the world. It isn't likely that an Indiana child of a single mother could easily go to Indiana University and earn a Ph.D. Personal ambition and talent are important, but, in my case, a committed government policy and generous programs made it possible. Political organizing for government action does matter.

Government and organized groups help dismantle institutional sexism and eliminate its economic consequences. William Hudnut, mayor of Indianapolis, has eloquently defended affirmative action for black males in the Indianapolis police department. His defense is certainly the most forceful of any Republican I am familiar with: the quality of police work improves if the force is integrated. Hudnut discovered the increase in quality after the Federal government required integration. Affirmative action helps an employer make good policies s/he would not otherwise likely make. However, there is a more fundamental aspect to affirmative action, one that affects the individual, not just the employer. Young women or blacks won't likely prepare for college, engineering, law and medical school without some guarantee that an affirmative action policy will be there to help them bypass the traditional sexist and racist procedures for admissions, hiring, and promotion. Affirmative action policies create real alternatives so that individuals can have real choices. To dwell on girls' upbringing to explain their enrollment in home economics courses and the existence and maintenance of job segregation is to rely on a blame-the-victim argument—an argument that lets the rest of us off the hook.

Another structural change that would improve the lives of women and men by expanding choices people can make is child care and paternal leave. The fact that the U.S. does not provide public child care for kids under five and that fathers are discouraged from taking on parental duties, creates an institutional hostility for and neglect of family life.

In the six years I have been in Indiana I have found that behind the particular complaints and demands I hear (and feel) is a sense of loss. I found a nostalgic yearning for a time when children were looked after by their mothers and men earned a family wage, as well as the contradicting realization that those days were stifling and unlikely to return. A Hoosier woman will most likely earn poverty wages in an unsatisfying job while pretending her children don't exist when she is at work and pretending her job doesn't exist when she is at home. She will take her own sick and vacation leave for her kids, sacrificing her own health care, rest, or her job.

Women have gained from working, but they have lost a great deal. Since children are deemed a private matter and women lack social and political clout, neither the government nor employers have compensated for the loss of labor faced by families when a woman goes to work. The cost of lost housework is borne mainly by mothers in families that can't afford housekeepers, restaurant meals, and quality child care.

On the other hand, a man's decision to start a household means never expecting the choice to spend time with his children. Time off for child care and parental leaves will not be recognized, even for emergencies; if you are a man, the measure of love for your family is defined by your employer: it is how much money, not time, you bring to them. Employers use fatherhood as a work incentive; men are asked to ignore their desires to work less and be with their children more.

Gender distinctions divide us and make men and women blind to our common interests as workers. Once while I was shopping in a women's clothing consignment shop I asked the young woman owner how an increase in the minimum wage would affect her. I had just completed a study that showed if the minimum wage had been $4.65 in 1986 South Bend workers would have earned $33 million dollars more—$22 million to women workers.

The owner quickly answered my question. She opposed raising the federal minimum wage because it would cause job loss. I asked her if she would have to cut hours if the minimum wage rose. She said no. As soon as she had a good worker, she regularly increased pay. Her employment needs were dictated by the demand for clothes, not wages.

I didn't ask her why, then, she opposed a measure that would raise local women's incomes and increase their ability to buy more clothes. I think I know the answer. This Hoosier woman had freed herself from wage work and joined the ranks of small business owners. She and other women owners identify with the male-dominated world of capital ownership. She didn't recognize that the male economy is becoming increasingly feminized and that she is part of the phenomenon. Her interests lie in increasing women's incomes. But because we hide the fact that most low wage workers are women and because employers, no matter how small, line up with the Chamber of Commerce, this woman did not act on her own behalf. Ideology replaced self-interest.

Eighty-eight percent of my profession, Ph.D. economists, and nine out of ten professors at the University of Notre Dame, are men. I live in Indiana and in a male economy. But when South Bend women protested and sought to improve their working lives in 1984, I finally recognized how statistics, economic policies, and ideology truly hid, ignored, and subordinated women. Indiana is not the show-me state, but it's a state that has shown me plenty. Its women have helped me see all sides of an economy.

❦ Michael Martone

LIVING DOWNTOWN

AFTER TEN years of living away from home, I took some time off from my job in Iowa to write a novel. I had most of a year, and I could have gone any place in the world. At the time I thought it was important to come back to Fort Wayne since that was where the novel was to be set and where my family still lived. So on a rainy fall day, I moved some books and papers along with a suitcase of clothes into a furnished efficiency apartment in the Poagston Arms on Berry Street downtown.

The Poagston is one of the few tower apartment houses built in Fort Wayne. Unlike the newer Three Rivers condominiums, the Poagston, built just after the Second World War, was never meant to be a luxury address. I supposed it had its big city pretensions at the beginning with its green awning shading the entry way, streamlined brick work and window treatment. It still retained the boom feeling of the war years when smart young women and working couples used to their independence and change in their pockets de-manded a convenient address, efficient appliances, and minimal housekeep-ing. When it was built, perhaps most everyone assumed that things would be growing downtown, that the Poagston was the first of many high-rises, a model for the city's future when Berry Street would be transformed into a scaled-down version of Park Avenue.

That's not the way things turned out, of course. When I moved in years later, the ten-story Poagston stood alone on its corner. The rest of the block had been cleared for parking lots the church across the street used and another one the Cadillac dealership wanted to abandon in a move out to the bypass. Berry Street was dotted with doctor's offices, more churches, a senior citizen center and housing complex, each with its own buffering parking lot, alter-nating to the center of the downtown. I could live in the Poagston now because it was cheap and there were several vacancies. It would be quiet. People, after all, hadn't wanted to live downtown. The future had people living in ground-hugging townhouses, a curious name, considering that they were ar-ranged in cul-de-sacs, satellites, beyond the bypass highways that no longer bypassed a thing, so far from town. The bright young women who had moved into the Poagston after the war were still there, my neighbors now, teachers mainly, nurses and legal secretaries who never married, close to retirement. They waited for the mail in the lobby as I moved in. They hadn't moved when the working couples had taken off to the suburbs when they were built. Strangely, it was not so much that the Poagston's time had come and gone— it always felt to me that the building's time had never come. It was like moving into someone's dream.

I never wrote the novel. The story was set during Prohibition and the Great Depression at the Irene Byron Tuberculosis Sanitarium outside Fort Wayne. Another reason I had chosen the Poagston was the senior center down the street. I imagined I could go in during the day when the men were wood-working or shooting pool and the women quilting or playing euchre and, with an introduction from my grandfather, start people talking about the times of the novel. I was especially interested in the downtown then, the way it stayed open all night, the lights of the dance halls and theaters, the sparks off the trolley wires, the spotlights on the mannequins in the windows of all the clothing stores. That downtown was one I could only imagine, pieced together from stories my grandfather remembered or what I could coax from my parents: the press of all those people who were downtown for all kinds of reasons, not just to work at the banks and courthouse but to shop, to hang out and to meet up and to change buses and street cars, to transfer from home to work, the whole city circulating through its heart each day. I wanted to sense a kind of ambient noise for the background of my book. But those things had faded from my informants' memories which had become as deserted as the downtown. Instead they recalled more personal moments, the ambiguous feelings of how hard it was but how happy. Mainly we sat around the big table shaking our heads at the prices of things, then each trying to top the last—the number of hotdogs for a quarter, the distance traveled on a dime, the pounds of candy for a penny.

This failure in my research method wasn't what doomed the novel. There were many things wrong with the idea, and I needed to write a bit of it to discover that. More interesting to me now was my original motivation to live downtown in the first place. Then I believed it might help to write about Fort Wayne while living in it. What I discovered, of course, is that the city I wanted to write about, the one I had been writing about for ten years, was not the city I looked at day after day from my fifth floor window in the

Poagston. After awhile I stopped working on the novel, started again on some stories about my Fort Wayne. But I also lived downtown in this other Fort Wayne and part of the time, the part when I wasn't dreaming, I walked the streets of the real city which seemed ghostly compared to what I knew it had been once. And it was a pale shadow of what I was dreaming.

The window looked west. In the distance, the red flashing lights of the television towers pulsed after the sunset. I counted seven towers, their lights all on unique sequences. I had no television, only a radio that tuned in WOWO, but the flashing lights seemed to have a patient binary intelligence, messages written in the air. A block away was St. Joe hospital where I had been born. It was close enough to see through the windows of the eastern facade into the rooms where the blue televisions seemed to float near the ceilings. I couldn't see the faces on the screens or the faces of the patients and nurses who moved from room to room. Below me on the other side of Fulton Street was the newspaper building parking lot that once had been Ed Harz's Standard station where my grandfather had moonlighted as an attendant all the time I was growing up. Then, at about this time of night, the nurses turned out the lights in the rooms, Ray tossed pizzas in his parlor next door (now also gone), and the *Journal* reporters filtered out of Henry's and crossed the street to work until deadline. That was about the time I'd come with my folks to pick up my grandfather from the station. He'd read the pumps and shut them off while we waited in the Olds. The lights went out. The twirling Standard sign stopped. Grandfather rattled the doors to make sure they were locked, then got in the car still smelling of gasoline and rubber. On some of those nights my parents would tease him about Betty, who lived at the Poagston. Betty liked to come over to sit inside the station and talk to my grandfather between customers. She would leave as grandfather locked up, waving to us in the car, then walk back across the street.

When I lived in the Poagston years later Betty was still there. She introduced me around in the lobby while we were all waiting for the mail carrier to finish sorting. "This is Jimmy's boy," she announced, never remembering she was skipping a generation. Other people used the lobby. There were offices on the ground floor and a music store, never open when I was around, its display window filled with huge brass tubas and sousaphones. When I turned 18 I came down to the Poagston to another office to register for the draft. During the war the bus left at night from Fulton Street with the new inductees.

Grandfather let them make collect calls on the station phone. Selective Service was gone now. The Vietnam veterans came in looking for the new office, and the women in the lobby pointed the way. The veterans' new office around the corner on Berry was always filled, like the lobby of the Poagston, with people waiting. Most strange were the brain doctor's patients. Their heads were bandaged elaborately or were asymmetrically shaved, mapped with flaps and sutures. They too were a bit distracted. I am probably remembering selectively now. The lobby of the Poagston couldn't always be populated by these brooding staring people. I was one of them, I admit, turned inward by writing every day and by worrying my own past as it cycled through my fiction. I remember it raining all the time. That can't be true. But the ceiling above Fort Wayne is often low and gray, the roof of clouds bearing down from the Great Lakes. Leaving the building on those days I stepped out on Berry where often it rained ashes. They were burning trash in the Poagston's incinerator.

My parents thought my living in the Poagston was crazy. If I had moved home to write, why not move all the way home? I reminded them that they had sold my bed years ago. The message had been clear enough then. We all knew that if I was going to work I couldn't actually live at home. Their house elicited only holiday behavior. Christmas could not go on that long. Still they felt they should say again that nobody lived downtown anymore.

They were partially correct. The old houses around the Poagston on the near west side of downtown had been cut up into doctor's offices or torn down for parking. A few of them had apartments for students of the art school or other young single people back from college who didn't want to move back in with their parents. There was some gentrification of the mansions and carriage houses but it was halfhearted. One day I watched them move a three-story turreted Victorian down Wayne Street in order to preserve it when the hospital needed more parking. It was to be used for doctors' offices. This neighborhood was mostly white. Then nearer in to downtown was the senior citizen housing project. On the near east side was the black neighborhood of single family houses. It moved around south away from the river toward the old Central High School, closed now. The students who lived in its district were bussed to the six high schools on the radiating outskirts of the city. People did live downtown. To my parents, to most of the city, it was just difficult for them to see this anymore. The people who lived downtown had become another type of ghost. Black families, the young and the old, single women and men. Even Vietnamese refugees were billeted that winter in the old Central Catholic High School. It was hard to integrate those definitions of living into greater Fort Wayne's sense of community. It was made worse because there were few reasons to come downtown anymore and few people did.

When the cognitive maps of a region are blank I imagine they may fill with frightening drawings of dragons, roughing in the terra incognita. I was crossing Fairfield one day walking downtown. The light had stopped traffic on the avenue, and as I walked in front of the cars, I heard the clicks of door locks. How I must have looked to these people when they were forced to stop and see me.

I felt very safe downtown mainly because I saw hardly anyone there at night after the banks closed. They cleared out at five, afraid of the emptiness that grows on the fear. Walking down Berry I could see the Fort Wayne Bank building. Most of the facade was sheathed in marble but from my angle I could see the rougher brick work of the side that had been hidden by an old hotel. I had watched them blow up the Van Ormen Hotel in what is the stunning state of the art now—that series of explosions ripping down the sides of the building, the way the floors float for a second before the squaring of their accelerating collapse takes over, the steaming pile of bricks and twisted reinforcing rod. One reason to make the trip downtown now is to see them blow it to bits. Downtown Fort Wayne was empty when I lived there. Whole blocks of parking lots were created as business moved away. A logic drove the destruction: parking would bring people back downtown. You can see the footsteps of the progress, the gaptooth architecture. And the new bank towers, as part of their international style, needed plazas and parks for people, their numbers still dwindling. There were fires that left holes when no one would invest. Temporary lots went in as the block lay fallow, a little outhouse hut near the gate. At night all the huts were empty, the cash register drawers left open to show me there was nothing to steal. When I lived in the Poagston the city was still destroying itself in order to save itself.

It got very cold after Thanksgiving and toward Christmas pipes burst in the Poagston. Parts of the building had no heat. I could see my breath as I sat in my tiny Murphy Kitchen and typed. The manager came around when I called after I could take no more. I remember he walked into the room, hugged himself and said, ''You know, in Europe this wouldn't be considered cold.'' It was cold in Indiana though. The frost on the window had little spy holes I melted with my fingers so I could look over at the hospital. I packed up to wait it out at my parents' where I would have an excuse for not finishing much work.

I now had to drive downtown for my walks at night. During the day I could ride the buses still running along the ancient trolley routes though the demographics of the city had shifted. Most of the other passengers I rode with were the clients of the State Training Hospital which is near my parents' house. We were all getting off at the old transfer corner across from Murphy's. Downtown Calhoun Street, even during the morning and evening rush, had been rendered desolate by its conversion to a transit mall. The big green buses alone on the bricked street lumbered up and idled as the clients dispersed to the departing buses that would take them to their jobs. We all waited in front of the boarded up store fronts while new buses collected. And then they were gone, the street empty without buses. I still couldn't bring myself to walk down the middle of it though you were encouraged to do so.

I haven't mentioned any villains behind the transforming of this cityscape into a kind of desert. The year I was born also saw the signing of the Defense Highway Act and the opening of the first McDonald's and Disneyland. It is too easy to anthropomorphize the car so I won't call it a villain even though the power of the machine to recast the world is overwhelming. The culture of the car had been pretty much established by the time I was born. The complete transformation took awhile longer. I have memories of shopping for school clothes at Pat's. My mother's hat and white gloves. And there are images of movies, photos from an old *Look* magazine featuring Fort Wayne as ''The Happiest Town in America'' where Calhoun Street is choked with people. On the streets of Fort Wayne years later I walked among ruins that were hard to see. It must have been like this for the Europeans when history began again in the late Middle Ages. Walking the streets of their own cities and passing the ruins, for the first time they realize that the Roman Empire has been dead for a long time. We believe we are the same people in the Happiest City but we are not; we are something else, something we cannot begin to see.

They found and renovated the electric Santa Claus that W & D's Department Store displayed each Christmas for years on the side of the old store. That Christmas I lived in the Poagston, they hung it again on the side of the Fort

Wayne Bank building. It was spectacular. I had never seen it before. Three stories, thousands of colored light bulbs, the ones on the runners of the sleigh strobing. Santa's whip cracked with light. Toys spilled from the pulsing bag. The display had been forgotten even when I was a child and my parents took me downtown to the new store to see the animated window displays. W & D's had been closed for years. Someone stumbled on Santa in a warehouse that was being torn down.

The parking lot below Santa was filled with cars, engines running, windshields smeared with lights. I watched the people inside craning to see up from under their car roofs the brilliant galaxy. A throbbing advertisement for a long gone store was now pure delight. Divorced from a forgotten past, it lit the sky like magic.

That same night horses and carriages appeared in the streets. The lights of the Santa Claus gleamed in the varnished finish of the phaetons and coupes. Some people got out of their cars and took carriage rides down Calhoun, the horses clopping through the red lights. I asked a driver wrapped in a rug when the rides had begun and why. She thought the time had come. A little like New York.

She said, "Other towns are doing it too."

"And what do people look at?" I asked.

"The lights," she said. The little twinkling lights the city had strung on the new trees planted along the transit mall.

A few months later, I moved out of the Poagston Arms. I said good-bye to my friends in the lobby. Time is always an unseen component of a place. I had sliced through this one moment of Fort Wayne. I took the train back out to Iowa. When I got there, it was night and it was spring.

❦ Kay Franklin

HURRY MOM, THE SUNSET IS UP!

Perspectives of Beverly Shores, Indiana 1969–1988

BEVERLY SHORES, Indiana: The "Tip O' The Lake" according to a commemorative license plate some of us sport on our cars; a picturesque town of
a thousand people—give or take a few; a town to which people are drawn
rather than born; a town with enough towering dunes, lake vistas, wooded
glades, and spectacular, rose-hued sunsets to keep the picture postcard people
in business for the next hundred years; and, since 1969, the town my family
calls home.

Hoosiers by transplant, we emigrated from Hyde Park, the University of
Chicago's neighborhood, after spending one glorious August in a rented lake
front cottage in Beverly Shores. The natural beauty of the dunes hooked us
for life during that holiday. We frolicked on Lake Michigan's wide, sandy
beaches, bicycled along the shaded paths, scuttled up bare moving dunes then
rolled or skidded down. As we picked wildflowers and wild blueberries, we
marveled—as did our fellow urbanites—at finding paradise only an hour from
Chicago. Not even the alewives dying and rotting on the beaches marred our
vision of heaven.

Like other Hyde Parkers before us, we bought some land overlooking the
lake, hired an architect, and drew up plans for a getaway cottage. Unlike
most of the others, however, we jettisoned the summer house idea, substituted
a year-round home with an unimpeded view of the Chicago skyline, and
relocated in Indiana.

In retrospect, our move seems uncharacteristically precipitous. Seduced
by the town's beauty and open space, the reassuring sight of unlocked bicycles
in the school yard and unguarded boats on the beaches, the clean and quiet
air, we succumbed to love at first sight. How little we knew of our new home
amazes me now.

We knew, of course, that two thirds of Beverly Shores belonged to the three-year-old Indiana Dunes National Lakeshore. We also knew that Congress had excluded 600 acres of the town's 3,200 from the new park, creating a privately owned "island" where our house stood. But we didn't know that the Lakeshore's existence fulfilled a dream Illinois and Indiana conservationists had held for fifty years, nor that its realization divided the town in more than geographic ways. We didn't know that during the long debate over preserving the dunes, townspeople had aligned themselves as pro-park or anti-park. That friendships and even some marriages had shattered over the controversy, that most social institutions in the town had broken down, and that those animosities would remain to color town life thereafter, we did not learn until much later.

With the exception of a few "hello, how are you" acquaintances, we didn't know a soul. We discovered for ourselves how to get along. Since Beverly Shores had few businesses, we shopped in Michigan City, an "All American City" several miles to the east. We delighted in the two movie houses, a dairy featuring old fashioned ice cream concoctions, a Jewish delicatessen that sold real rye bread and bagels, and a shiny new indoor shopping mall; of those, only the shopping mall remains.

We soon learned that our children, then aged eleven, nine and three, would complete sixth grade in the six-room Beverly Shores School and then go, via school bus, to Michigan City for junior and senior high school. Our all too casual inquiries revealed that people liked the ambience of the elementary school and possibly the education as well. That only 40 percent of the high school students went on to college, and of those, over 90 percent to Indiana institutions, seemed noteworthy, but too far in the future to concern us.

We didn't know much about the people back in 1969. Self-selected for autonomy, they prided themselves on being different, out of the main stream. They thrived on independence and self-sufficiency, on their ability to tolerate isolation yet coalesce when the occasion arose. While the natives didn't go out of their way to meet a new neighbor, most responded to our needs for information and companionship. The little school, under the wrecker's ball as I write, provided a social focus for me as well as for my children. Our community exemplified a healthy mix of incomes, ages, education, backgrounds, sexual preferences, occupations, and interests. Although we've had a sizeable Lithuanian population, few members of minority groups have ever lived here. Artists, writers, architects, professors, psychoanalysts, and other professionals swelled the population in the summer; some of them joined the steel workers, mechanics, carpenters, and beach combers to live year 'round. The town exhibited a rural character, when we first came, even though many of its inhabitants donned suits and ties and commuted daily to work in Chicago.

We still divide ourselves along the same axes that we did then: summer people and year-round; "rich people on the lakefront" and all the rest; supporters of the National Lakeshore and those opposed; residents in the "island" and lease-back holders in the park; those who work in Chicago and those who work everywhere else; Republicans and Democrats—and, as of the 1987 Town Board election, Independents.

We didn't know much about the lake either. Separated from the beach by a parallel road, our house overlooked 100 yards of sand fringed with pebbles at water's edge. From our location, we could walk the beaches (which almost all belong to the National Lakeshore) for miles; we assumed we would always be able to do so. Unknown to us, however, the lake level had been inching its way up from a record low level in 1964, although by 1969 it had not increased appreciably. Had we thought to ask, we might have learned that in the late fifties the water level had risen so high that several houses had fallen in, and that our lake front road had once stretched three miles farther—all the way to Michigan City.

I realize now how much that mammoth fresh water sea dominates our lives. For those of us who live north of the first dune ridge, particularly, the lake affects our climate, our weather, our comfort, our recreation, our spirits, our safety, and our property values.

The lake rises and falls according to precipitation levels around the Great Lakes. Evaporation caused by heat and wind also plays a part. Nevertheless, its swings remain the stuff of myth. Some local people maintain that the ups and downs occur in ten-year cycles; others talk of seven-year rotations. Scientists warn that an impending "mini-ice age" or the advent of a "greenhouse effect" may affect the lake in unanticipated ways. International politics, which regulates diversion of water in and out of the Great Lakes, impacts its highs and lows as well.

Regardless of the cause, changes in water levels affect us profoundly. My first look at the devastation resulting from high water remains with me still. It occurred in 1973 when, according to the U.S. Army Corps of Engineers, the lake had risen about a foot above its previous high. By then, the beaches

looked narrow even on a calm day, and the gentlest of winds thrust the waves
into abrasive contact with the toe of the foredune.

That November, always a bad month for storms, the north wind arrived
early and settled in for a long, unwelcome visit. Day and night for four days
it howled. Despite locked windows and drawn blinds the noise hammered in
our ears. The waves, propelled by fifty to sixty-knot winds, reached moun-
tainous proportions. Like ravenous giants, they gobbled up the dune across
the road, gulping down a foot or two of marram grass and sand with each
insatiable bite. We had not wanted drapes in the living room; we wanted
nothing to come between us and our magnificent view. But that November I
wished I could pull a cord and obliterate the sight of such destruction.

Storms throughout the years have produced their own Beverly Shores
history. I first encountered the suddenness of their violence on a peaceful
August afternoon not long after we arrived. Some women acquaintances and
I were lazing at the beach about three blocks from home, watching our children, perfecting our tans, gossiping, enjoying the sun, the sand, and the water.
Toward the end of afternoon, the sky began to darken, turning an angry
greenish black. All at once, without any conversation about the weather, the
women rose, packed up their paraphernalia and their kids, said good-bye and
scattered.

The instant I reached home, I rushed to close my ground floor windows
even though I could not feel the slightest breeze or see a ripple on the lake.
Somewhere between the first window and the last, the wind whipped up. By
the time I got upstairs, the gale was blowing so hard that the house creaked
and shook, and sawdust spewed from our cedar ceilings; I thought I wouldn't
have the strength to get that final window shut.

For a long while, the 1973 St. Patrick's Day storm held first place as the
fiercest anyone remembered. It relinquished its position February 8, 1987.
On that Sunday a combination of the highest lake level ever recorded, sus-
tained winds clocked at eighty knots, an inadequate ice shelf (the annual
buildup of ice along the beach that protects the dune from winter's ravages)
and rapidly falling temperatures produced a storm of monumental scope.
Worse yet, a seiche—a kind of tidal wave that occurs on inland lakes—
pushed even more water toward Beverly Shores.

The next day, I ventured on foot to the area hardest hit—Lake Front Drive
about a mile east of us. The storm had made the road, what was left of it,

impassable. Waves had leapt the beach, breaking far from their source, freezing as they receded. They had hurled tree trunks, railroad ties, and telephone poles onto the road then encased them in tombs of ice. Despite this chaos, the scene looked gorgeous. Ice covering every surface glittered and sparkled in the sun.

We don't fixate on bad weather only; almost every other kind preoccupies us too, especially in summer. In our household, for example, wind direction and temperature determine issues of vital importance. Shall we drink our morning coffee on the front porch or the back? Is it warm enough to bring our cup to the deck, or would the beach make a nicer spot to sip our brew? Shall we jog today or walk? Bicycle or swim? Take the camera, the bird book, the wildflower book, the tree book and go for a hike? Will the waves enhance a sail or will the south wind and humidity fill the boat with stinging flies?

And where shall we spend the close of that summer day? Usually, unless the temperature pushes into the nineties, we watch the sunset—ever new—from our front porch. We still hear the echo of our three-year-old, impatient to share that great orange slide. ''Hurry!'' her voice still shouts, ''Hurry Mom, the sunset is up!''

Because our setting propels us toward the outdoors, we take our seasons seriously and wait eagerly for signals of their change. Everyone else looks for the first flower, migrating bird, mushroom, or hint of frost, but I rely on a different index.

Insects, whose coexistence I have come to tolerate if not welcome, presage the evolving year for me. I don't need any groundhog to tell me when to kiss winter good-bye. When ants man their battle stations in my kitchen I suspect that hepaticas, spring beauties, and marsh marigolds will soon defy the wind chill and brazen their way through the ready earth. Wood roaches, country cousins to the despised urban cockroach, represent an even surer sign of spring. Some years as early as February, they move right in along with the ants. Their coppery stained glass wings glistening on rare patches of sunlight tell me, despite the evidence of all my senses, that winter will soon head out of town.

As soon as it's warm enough to open the windows, the no-see-'ems invade. Black specks too small to see through any plane of my trifocals, they raise welts as big as golf balls when they don't get a fair share of our bed. And itch? Poison ivy and mosquito bites together can't compete with the no-see-'ems. We have never figured out why some years they make a meal out of me while in others they feast on my mate. Seldom do both of us suffer their wrath at the same time. Mercifully.

Summer brings out still more of the troops: Junebugs, flies, mosquitoes, spiders, daddy longlegs, fire flies, grasshoppers, crickets, lady bugs, katydids, water beetles, hair bees, gnats, dragon flies. On sultry nights even though nobody has left the door open and none of the screens has a hole, the living room suddenly fills with flying creatures. Buzzing, swooping, whirring, possibly responding to an impending storm, they blanket the windows and hover about the lights. Those that come too close to bulbs pop and hiss as their bodies contact the heat. Then, just as suddenly, the wind shifts from south to north and the flying circus disappears as rapidly as it came.

When the fruit flies come, I know I am seeing the last of the good weather for another year. Pesky and persistent, they swarm over the last offerings of orchard and garden. Meals become open warfare between human and insect diners. I must cover or refrigerate everything edible; a drop of juice splashed on the counter encourages them to invite the whole family for a party. We can't even take to drink. A glass of wine covered with floating corpses soon loses its appeal. Were it not for the fruit flies, I would want winter never to come. After a few weeks of fighting them, I'm ready.

With the coming of fall, we get down to the business of doing something about our water. Each house in Beverly Shores has its own well and septic system, and most of us have perpetual trouble with one or the other or both. The state of one's well makes for rousing conversation on any occasion. Sometimes discussion focuses on the color of the water which ranges from yellow to brown with most shades in between, sometimes on its taste which ranges from lousy to undrinkable. The few people who have tapped into Artesian wells never fail to lord their clear, sweet-tasting water over the rest of us. Other times we exchange notes on the caliber of the well men we've used, how many times we've changed the well point, whether we've replaced the two inch pipe with a four, if we can blame the pump, the point, or the plumbing for the inevitable lack of pressure. We love to talk about the depth of our wells and how close to the clay layer we've drilled. Divining rods versus other water-finding methods and the merits of competing water treatment systems make satisfying topics too.

Until we switched to a four inch well, an improvement a succession of well-fixers assured us we couldn't achieve, we had nonstop water problems. For the better part of our children's lives, we all took scheduled showers, ran only one water appliance at a time, and waited until the toilet tank filled before trying to get water out of the tap.

One frigid Thanksgiving our water stopped completely. After much frantic calling, we located a well man who deigned to come out and look at it. He drove his rig up our summer neighbor's driveway, the only place from which he had access to our well. (A design flaw both architects seem to have overlooked.) The rig developed problems and ceased to work for five days. While the drillers tinkered with it, bringing in a part every once in awhile to try to get it going, my husband ran our neighbor's water into our system through a garden hose. I thought it wouldn't work, but it did. We spent our Thanksgiving holiday nursing the hose, wrapping it in blankets, tending it like a pampered child, waiting either for the cold snap to break or the rig to get fixed.

Wells and septic systems have their advantages too. They have, over the years, kept the housing density low in Beverly Shores. Surrounding lake front communities with access to city water and sanitation have more houses built on smaller lots. Our zoning ordinance, which now requires 20,000 square feet to build a single family house, would be vulnerable in the courts if we had city water and sewers. We can insist on large lots because smaller ones compromise public health and safety. Without that basis, developers lusting to build on smaller parcels might prevail. While the idea of city water tempts me every time I turn on the tap, I'll stick with my well in the interest of protecting our precious open space.

Just as Lake Michigan dominates our natural scene, the overarching presence of the National Lakeshore dominates our civic and personal lives. Coping with the implications of park/town coexistence has topped our agenda since the dunes debate first impinged on Beverly Shores in the late fifties. No weightier issue has yet come along to take its place.

In 1958, unable to find an Indiana sponsor, dunes preservationists persuaded Illinois's senator, Paul Douglas, to lead their effort to create a national park in the dunes. They believed that the area's natural beauty and scientific uniqueness met the National Park Service's test of national significance. The fear that industrial and residential incursion would soon destroy this valuable resource gave a sense of urgency and solidarity to the preservation effort.

Many in Beverly Shores joined the Save the Dunes Council and lobbied hard for the proposed park and for the town's inclusion. They willingly agreed to sell their homes to the government and lease them back for twenty-five years. Others supported the park yet chose to keep their homes in perpetuity, a provision permitted under the proposed legislation. But not everybody went along; a number of residents vociferously opposed including Beverly Shores in a national lakeshore. They sided with the entire political establishment of Indiana maintaining that outsiders should not determine the fate of the dunes or of the town. These opponents felt able to protect the place they loved without the help of Douglas or the interference of the federal government.

Faced with lack of consensus in Beverly Shores, Congress imposed a Solomonic decision on the 1966 lakeshore legislation: Cut the baby in thirds—two thirds in the park; one third—the "island"—left out. In so deciding, our legislators created a jurisdictional monster which has perpetuated dissension among townspeople and caused unanticipated, ongoing headaches for the national park's managers.

Recognizing the difficulties ahead, Beverly Shores residents pulled together for a brief moment in the early seventies and supported expansion legislation which called for including the "island" in the lakeshore. Twice more Congress rejected the "island." Instead they rethought the original homeowner provisions and passed new legislation that required residents in the park to sell their homes after all. Such arbitrary treatment reactivated anti-park sentiments and destroyed our momentary consensus forever.

Nobody, least of all Congress, foresaw the problems the Beverly Shores solution would create. A bonafide conflict of interest between park and town resulted, one which no amount of good will can entirely erase: The Lakeshore must obey a mandate to develop its Beverly Shores holdings and make facilities accessible to an increasingly large population of park visitors; the town must protect the privacy and property of its people from the impact of increased traffic, litter, noise, and crime.

Furthermore, we must beef up our services in the face of a rapidly declining tax base. When the leases run out, the Park Service will demolish the houses—if it has the money. Beverly Shores will lose the property tax revenue and we will have an even bigger problem maintaining town services than we do now. Increased construction of new homes in the "island" will not compensate for the loss, despite the claims of developers, because when the number of houses increases, the State of Indiana lowers tax rates for each of us rather than increasing the total monies the town can collect.

Too often we lock horns with a plethora of governmental jurisdictions. In addition to our town and the county governments, we contend with the Indiana Department of Natural Resources (the Indiana Dunes State Park borders us on the west), the Department of the Interior, the National Park Service, the United States Coast Guard, and the Army Corps of Engineers.

Having to confront such problems has produced certain benefits. Town organizations, which died during the park struggle of the fifties and sixties, have reawakened. We now boast a thriving residents' association whose newsletter, except for rumor the only information source in town, keeps its members abreast of everything from congressional action to new recipes. The ABSR, as it's called, protects residents' interests, holds social events, and raises funds. We have a woman's club that does good works and raises funds, a volunteer fire department that puts out fires and raises funds, a police action league that boosts police morale and raises funds, and a Lithuanian club that probably raises funds too. We also have a Catholic church that serves mass and pancake breakfasts. Catholics attend the masses; the whole town attends the breakfasts.

Most of the town shows up at the annual Firemen's Ball held on the Saturday closest to the Fourth of July. The summer people wouldn't miss it. They dress up in country chic and stand around the fire station watching us natives. The band plays any kind of music as long as it's loud, and the ladies' auxiliary serves brats to go with the beer, the booze, and the band.

Our organizations also tackle seemingly hopeless situations. In December, 1986, for instance, when beach erosion threatened the west end of Lake Front Drive, they banded together to spearhead a sandbagging brigade. For an entire weekend residents turned out in the cold to fill and place sandbags against the eroding dune. Someone with a good grounding in P. R. contacted the Chicago and South Bend TV stations who came with mini-cams to record our efforts for the six o'clock news. Our woman's club set up a van and gave away hot dogs and hot coffee to the workers. A Brownie troop from the neighboring town of Chesterton read about our plight in the paper and came to help. Everyone, from men and women in their seventies to young children, contributed to the success of the save-the-road effort.

Local politics always plays a serious role in Beverly Shores life. Until this year we've had two parties—the Republicans who generally oppose the National Lakeshore, and the Democrats who mostly support it. Town Board candidates on the Republican slate either pretend the Lakeshore doesn't exist or boast that they will outshout it and bring it down to size. Democratic candidates advocate cooperation with the Lakeshore, just as long as it doesn't interfere with town interests. Familiar issues also spice campaign rhetoric regularly every four years: water, speed limits, loose dogs, parking, garbage, zoning, and ordinance enforcement. All candidates worry about money—of which the town has less and less—and where to get more of it.

In most town board elections upwards of 70 percent of those registered turn out to vote. Since we've lived here, about half the elections have gone to the Republicans and half to the Democrats. This past November, we fielded an Independent slate in addition to the other two, giving us almost as many people running as voting. The Independents won by a huge number and will probably soon come down to earth and realize that they can't accomplish much more than did the other two parties when they had their chance.

In addition to the elected town board, we have an appointed plan commission, a building commissioner, a board of zoning appeals, a site selection committee, and a park board. I served on the plan commission during the four years we wrote a new zoning ordinance. First we held a fund-raising party. We took $1,000 from the proceeds and hired a planning consultant from Valparaiso University. Then, to make sure we didn't break any laws, we recruited a committee of volunteer lawyers from among our Chicago summer people. Using the zoning ordinances from every hamlet in northwest Indiana as models, the commission—novices all—plowed into the unknown.

A noisy minority of townspeople disapproved of our efforts and came to every meeting with their lawyers to heckle and boo. Sometimes, when especially riled, they spat at our president. They even sued us, if I remember correctly. Those who favored our positions came to the meetings to cheer us on. I count those four years as the most disagreeable I have ever spent here. Nevertheless, our do-it-yourself zoning still works today.

Beverly Shores also has a dark side, one that most of us don't like to think about. We have had at least four murders here. In one case, unknown intruders killed an elderly couple who lived in an isolated summer cottage. In another, a desperate, demented woman convinced her teenage son to "accidentally" shoot his father. Everybody knew that family. They owned our only gas station for awhile; the youngster went to kindergarten with our daughter before being transferred to a fundamentalist Christian school. Just two days ago, police discovered a decomposing body, not yet identified, in a house adjoining the highway. Cause of death? Bludgeoning with a sharp object, probably an axe. We've also had several epidemics of arson. In one year eleven houses burned to the ground; in another year, five. Because many once stood on federal property, the FBI came to look into the tragedies. To the best of my knowledge neither they nor our local investigators ever found out who set the fires.

Much as we hate to admit it, profound changes have come to Beverly Shores. The real world impinges on our isolated jewel, creating pressures both from within and without. Now that they know with certainty that the "island" will never become part of the Lakeshore, realtors and developers are vying for every buildable lot. Individual land owners are joining in, haunting the tax sales and the county auditor's office hoping for property to acquire or barter. Houses and building sites now sell for prices undreamed of only a year ago. Just as we suffered when the long steel corridor between Detroit and Chicago corroded during the last decade, we share now in the rediscovery of the Indiana-Michigan lake front as a prized recreational resource.

The new prosperity, although welcome, has changed our character from rural to exurban. Building costs and zoning requirements prohibit the modest, unheated summer dwellings that dotted our landscape twenty years ago. With grander houses has come a different population, older, more urban, more affluent. Most of the newcomers, owners of primary homes elsewhere, are more likely to display a Mercedes than a pickup in the driveway, or rely on a sophisticated alarm system instead of the business end of a dog. We have lost much of the heterogeneity that made us so unique.

The new part-timers, like the summer people who have loved Beverly Shores for a generation, come to play, not to live. Although they generously donate money and goods when asked, they do not offer what we need the most: hour power and votes. And who can blame them? They man the barricades where they really live and do not come to Beverly Shores to confront more problems.

The increasing popularity of the Lakeshore—visitation up 28 percent between 1987 and 1988—means increasing impact on our slender resources. Within the year we will have a federally owned picnic area designed for 100 people at one end of our main street, and not long after, a major Lakeshore campground at the other. As the lease-back houses come down, our tax base will decline leaving us to substitute ingenuity for cold, hard cash.

Will we be up to the challenge? We have no other choice. Battling giants doesn't scare us; we have practiced, now, for a very long time. Though we often do not agree, Beverly Shoresites have tremendous energy and creativity to harness; we also know how to make a great deal of noise. Long experience with pushing political buttons hasn't hurt us either. If we have learned to live with nature's caprices, with a judicious mix of cooperation and compromise, we may yet learn to live with the federal government.

We'll have to, I guess, because few of us can imagine living anywhere else. Enhanced by twenty years of reflection, the values that propelled us to Beverly Shores—closeness to nature, love of the outdoors, the wish for a quiet, independent life—still wield great power. For us, the privilege of living in so beautiful a place makes all the difficulties worth while.

❦ William O'Rourke

THE LITERATURE OF PLACE AND NO PLACE

THE TOWN where I live, South Bend, Indiana, has an identity problem. Several, in fact. Some are geographic. The Chamber of Commerce uses a hyphenated label, South Bend–Mishawaka, as a name, as well as the term *Michiana*. Mishawaka is the town adjacent to South Bend, to the east. It has a number of distinctions, including a building boom of malls and car dealerships along Grape Road. (This Grape has many vines now, all of them bulging with ripe American shopping varietals.) "Michiana" is derived from the blending of state borders. Michigan is a stone's throw from South Bend.

The Michigan/Indiana conflicts—taxes, time zones, lotteries, and liquor sales—are other versions of South Bend's own town/gown split, between Notre Dame (itself a "town") and South Bend. During the 1988 NCAA basketball tournament banners emblazoned "South Bend, Indiana" were replaced for a televised game with ones reading "Notre Dame, Indiana 46556," a sorry display of zip code jingoism.

Other sorts of identity problems are, perhaps, more serious. Some are economic. "Dying rust-belt town" is a label that is used. Heavy manufacturing has been departing for quite a while. South Bend's population growth has stalled. The city's government has tried to attract new businesses to replace those that have left. Once famous for building Studebakers, South Bend is now a regional center of service industries: hospitals, banks, shopping.

The South Shore railroad still rolls from Chicago to South Bend. And, since South Bend is some one hundred miles by car from Chicago, it is under the gravitational sway of that large metropolis; it bends the orbits of South Bend residents in many varied ways. Those who live at the edges (of continents, of states) often find their communities hosting alien influences.

An economist I know is of the opinion that the midwest produces and the two coasts consume. This may well be the case and it certainly is true when it comes to the production of middle America's writers and artists.

I consider myself a child of the midwest. So much so, I declared it on the first page of my first novel, *The Meekness of Isaac*: "As a child of the Middle West there was nothing to do but leave it, for it is the center of the country and any direction in which you may go is away.'' Away I indeed went, repeating the same journey many American writers made throughout the twentieth century, from the center to the edge. What is different now, toward the end of the century, is that so many are returning, for reasons both profound and simple, reasons that I will attempt to sketch.

Being a ''serious'' writer in the late twentieth century means one of three things. You come from wealth or have married it, you struggle, or you teach. The modifier ''serious'' is a tricky one. It is now generally used to be the antonym of ''commercial.'' Commercial implies that you make money by writing. Serious implies no such thing; if anything it implies just the opposite.

In 1981 Herbert Mitgang reported in the *New York Times* the results of a survey which showed that the average income (from writing) of half of American writers was less than $5,000 a year. Just what consitutes a writer was defined as ''a contemporary American writer who had had at least one book published.'' This income figure is disputable, but if the survey had been limited to contemporary American novelists the amount would not be doubted—though, perhaps, as a median figure, rather than average. Stephen King and a few others would skew the numbers. Regardless, very few novels earn what they cost to write, if they are ''serious.'' Most are bankrolled by trust funds, wealthy acquaintances, or the nonwriting toil of the writer. Universities are subsidizing a great many commercial publishers, since the writers who publish with them could not afford to write without the employment of teaching. This is both good and bad.

In my midwestern youth, the cliché I grew up with (I was born in 1945) was, ''If you can't do, teach.'' It is my contention that my generation of writers can do—and does—both. When I graduated from the University of Missouri–Kansas City in 1968 and took myself to New York for graduate school at Columbia University I had no idea that I was participating in one of the literary movements of my generation: the growth of graduate writing programs throughout the land. (Columbia's had just started.) This, too, was both good and bad.

In 1968 my generation had the experience of preceding generations to shape it—and whatever myth-making about writers' lives that had been passed down over the years. One myth that was still potent was the writer as primitive, the self-educated man of experience. Doubtless the Beat Generation of the 1950s had something to do with this, except that many of the Beat Generation's primary figures had come from and had orbited around the same Columbia University I was attending in 1968. But the notion was hard to shake: writers somehow were educated by life, not in classrooms (either/or always, rather than the actual *both*). Even Thomas Wolfe—who had seemed to my younger self a representative primitive as I thought of them—had gone to graduate classes at Harvard (in playwriting!). Hemingway, one of the few twentieth century American writers of prominence without some college experience, was a doctor's son and most certainly could have gone to college.

The mushrooming of graduate writing programs during the seventies was something new. Though the Midwest had been associated with—and even responsible for—schools of writing (more literally than figuratively because of the history of the Iowa Writing Workshop), until the end of the sixties there had been mainly migration. Young writers (to-be) would come from the coasts to the Midwest for instruction and the midwesterners would head for the coasts. In both cases, the *strangeness* was salubrious. Since the beginning of the seventies writing programs have prospered everywhere (almost everywhere). The journey of the American writer is no longer just along the simple east-west axis, but is determined by a more complicated vortex of destinations and departures.

There are a number of large cultural forces at work, as well as the more individual tensions of particular personalities at play, that fashion the current situation. America is moving, like it or not, into a postliterate age. The aural/visual culture is now more dominant than the print culture. We are presented with the paradox of a golden age—in terms of numbers—of writers, but it is no golden age of readers. At least 50,000 "books" are published each year, but the ratio of readers to population—readers of certain sorts of literature—has become smaller. (The number of first novels published in 1928 was roughly that of the number published in 1978, according to *Library Journal*, a little more than a hundred. It is now a little more than three hundred.) Reading is a finite thing. It takes time to read and all that competes for people's time and attention is remarkable.

The current dispute over certain changes in course reading lists at universities (like the case of Stanford's Western Civ: what constitutes a great book, etc.) is symptomatic of many things, but one uncontestable thing it points to is the fact that very few people read the same books. Many people see the same TV shows and movies. If there are now more books being published the likelihood decreases that people will read the same ones. Excess can produce a babble even more efficiently than general ignorance. As the number of magazines and books increases, the one outlet of reading that declines is the number of newspapers available in any city. This situation benefits the status quo in a number of depressing ways: the overeducated are never speaking the same language to each other and the undereducated stand less of a chance of becoming well informed.

Writers may wonder where they are coming from, the effect of place on their work, but they also are concerned with where they are going, what sort of place their work might have in the culture.

The postliterate age is having definite effects on the subject of place. In the past, regional writers, in Tom McGuane's remark, were writers who collected "funny phrases." A regional writer these days can acquire uniqueness through his or her parochialism. If s/he only knows or chronicles one place, s/he is protected, safe down deep in the regional cellar from the cyclone of American homogenization. The paradox of our culture is the acquiring of sameness (the *malling* of the collective psyche) contending with the impulse toward eccentricity (territorial signs marking more limited kinships). Geography still holds dominion over some of this; individuals, chameleonlike, often want to blend into the landscape, regardless of the idiosyncrasies of region.

But the general situation in 1988 of the writer in these United States makes the "Indiana" writer a different sort of creature than s/he might have been in the not-too-distant past. In the reference volume *Indiana Authors and Their Books, 1967–1980*, the compiler, Donald E. Thompson, makes a number of salient points. The first concerns what is needed to qualify as an Indiana author: one must have been "born in Indiana or have lived in the state for at least twenty to twenty-five years." Given that criterion, I do not qualify, and will not, it seems, for at least another twelve years.

The accident of birth conveys inalienable rights, but the accruement of citizenship requires time served. No doubt this is to eliminate an infestation of intellectual carpetbagging (L. L. Bean-bagging?) by gypsy writers caravaning across the country. But what is interesting about such rules of entitlement (and they are common) is that they are completely antithetical in reasoning. They announce a kind of understanding of the power of chance and the power of hard work. You can either be lucky or steadfast. So a writer who is born in Indiana, but spends most if not all of his life elsewhere is an Indiana author, whereas one who writes a number of books in Indiana over a span of, say, nineteen years is not. What such an irrational rule points to is a fact: we ascribe such a title not to a person so much as an idea—our presumptions of what that idea is. So, if a future author was born in Indiana, Indiana-ness is in that writer's blood, or forebears (or transfused by the trauma of birth, if the parents happened to be driving through). It is a genuflection to the magical properties of being born. The other takes more sweat and tears, two decades for the necessarily humdrum, quotidian osmosis to occur.

Of course, there are other ways to classify writers. Again, the idea of *place* in literature is an old one; not a few volumes have been devoted to it. What would Joyce be without Dublin? But there are plenty of unnameable Irish writers who have written about Dublin. What is wished for by proponents of place is that a writer of genius (or great talent) occupies and writes about one. (And, by doing so, celebrating and honoring the place—or, at least, bringing it retroactive glory or notoriety.) When one wonders what northern Michigan (or Oak Park, Illinois) did to Hemingway, one is asking essentially psychological questions, as if one is raised by trees, by nature, by cement and brick. One is, in a manner of speaking—or writing.

Writers are often contradictory personalities. Opposing attributes are required for certain sorts of composition: you must be curious and adventurous, but also have the capacity to remain in one place and do solitary work. And many writers have found it impossible to write about the place they are presently in; perhaps this differs with genre. The poet John Matthias has described (in "Poetry of Place," the *Southern Review*) why he hadn't written about the St. Joseph river, so close to hand, though he has written of three rivers in England: "I think the reason is that while the St. Joseph is rich with associations that might stimulate another poet . . . for me it is associated entirely with the kind of daily grind that prevents poetry from being written. . . . It is the river I cross in my car to go to work." John Matthias would qualify as an Indiana poet, since he has lived in the state twenty years. (Though his depiction could describe a literature of anti-place, a not-uncommon genre for midwestern writers, most often practiced by novelists: one thinks of Sinclair Lewis, Sherwood Anderson, and Indiana's own Theodore Dreiser.) Ernest Sandeen, another true Indiana poet (over forty years in South Bend), finds it otherwise. His poetry is suffused with the sustenance of place: "It smelled of old secrets unearthed'' (from ''Gardening Through the Ages.'') What Robert Frost was to New England, Sandeen is to our Midwest. Sonia Gernes, the poet and novelist, in residence for more than twelve years, has learned, she writes in her poem ''Back Home in Indiana,'' the ''passions of the landlocked heart.'' But Anthony Kerrigan, the poet and award winning translator, likes to call this corner of Indiana where he has resided for nearly ten years ''Siberia, U.S.A.''

I have my own experience (as well as accounts of others), but with regard to fiction writers of a certain sort, leaving presents you with immediate perspective, the distance required to see clearly. One definition that can be employed to separate nonfiction and fiction is this: nonfiction is written from fact, fiction is written from memory. When one writes fiction one is remembering and the event takes place in one's head, not out one's window (though it may have taken place out the window some time before).

When I lived in New York City I found it difficult to write fiction there. There were many reasons for that, doubtless. One was the contrast of the city itself, the great metropolis, its hulking heroic materialism, to my own work. I would leave my small apartment on Charles Street and see the twin towers of the World Trade Center looming. It was difficult not to let the fragile paragraphs of the day be crushed by such sights. New York City is more a place of performance than creation.

I wrote a great deal about New York City in my second novel, *Idle Hands*, but I wrote about it in South Hadley, Massachusetts. I did not begin the writing of my third novel, *Criminal Tendencies*, till I began teaching in Indiana at the University of Notre Dame. *Criminal Tendencies* is set in Key West, Florida. New York City is engraved in my memory; Key West, a place I visited on and off for a decade, is also similarly etched. (Though I cannot be a New York author, or a Florida author, either, since I have not lived in either place twenty years. I haven't lived anywhere twenty years yet, not an uncommon circumstance for writers of my generation. I was born in Chicago, but moved from there when I was four. Am I an Illinois writer?)

But I have found that where you write is as important as what you write about, because the great difficulty is the writing itself. Does the place permit you to write? That is, to me, more the *literature of place* than the usual conferred meaning of the term: not the place you write about, but the place that lets you write. New York City did many things for me, gave me ten years of full life and higher education, but I was able only to write short pieces there. The life was too difficult, too hectic. New York City breeds wonderful nonfiction, journalism; the novels, books of memory, not fact, tend to be written outside of it. (Thomas Wolfe, you remember, wrote in Brooklyn, looking homeward to North Carolina using the jagged skyline of New York City as a sharp spur to memory.)

Donald E. Thompson in *Indiana Authors* discusses remarks by R. E. Banta found in the first (1916) volume of the series, " . . . one central theme is that Indiana has produced a proportionately larger number of writers than any other state in the union. . . . " Indeed, the three reference volumes include 6,819 authors, quite a harvest. A current reference volume, *A Directory of American Poets and Fiction Writers 1987–1988* (with its own not too dissimilar criteria for inclusion—it leaves out the aspiring and the lightly published), includes the names and addresses of sixty contemporary poets and fiction writers living in Indiana. (Doubtless, an equal number could have been missed.)

The states with the highest numbers of poets and fiction writers might be guessable: New York State has more than nine hundred listed, though New York City alone accounts for more than half of that number. California is second with over three hundred, followed by Massachusetts with somewhat less than two hundred. Though not necessarily an accurate count, the *Directory* provides what I take to be correct proportions, state by state. Of Indiana's neighbors, Ohio and Illinois have some twenty-five more listed than our state's sixty, Michigan a bit more, Kentucky far less. The proportion of writers one finds has something to do with the number of writing positions at institutions of higher learning in each state. Those with more will have more writers, for the reasons I've mentioned earlier, the burgeoning of writing programs throughout the land during the past two decades, which allows states to keep the writers they have and lure others. Big cities play a role: writers will be found in Boston, San Francisco, Chicago, as well as in states with geographic attractions, coastlines, mountain ranges, charged landscapes and associations (New Mexico has more writers listed than Kansas.)

Well, things have changed since 1816–1916, the period Banta was considering. We have moved into a postliterate era and the reasons why writers come and go, or go and come, have altered. But the Midwest tends to honor production and it is not always clear to the population what writers produce.

One reason Indiana has literary roots, Thompson points out, is Richard Cordell's observation about "the proximity of Cincinnati and Lexington as early periodical publishing centers and the later establishment of the Bobbs-Merrill Company in Indianapolis."

New York City tends to hold writers in somewhat higher regard because it is clear that even poets and fiction writers make money for the city's inhabitants. It is the publishing center of the country; all those concerned know what writers do. But elsewhere, where the industry is not so large (or nonexistent, especially for poetry and fiction), writers do not seem to be producers, or are not seen to be adding anything to the region, either good or bad. In South Bend, I am a professor at Notre Dame; everyone understands that. If I say I am a writer I am only presented with quizzical expressions and calls for explanation.

But, yet, a number of midwestern states have taken the time to honor their writers of late, though they are writers with enduring reputations and some decades dead. I was the first James Thurber writer at the Thurber House in Columbus, Ohio, in 1984, and a couple of years later was invited to speak at a Literary Heritage conference in Springfield, Illinois, where a reception was held at the poet Vachel Lindsey's house, which is open for public inspection. In Missouri there is Mark Twain's home in Hannibal, which I saw as a youth and which gave me the impression that writers could be held in esteem.

My connection to Indiana, whether or not I become an "Indiana" author (by virtue of residing here two decades), is already intricate. Though my most recent novel, *Criminal Tendencies,* is set in Key West, there are moments that owe their origin to the back roads around South Bend and Elkhart, Indiana, to the atmosphere engendered by the sight of satellite dishes squatting next to trailer homes on shaved plots of domesticated land surrounded by fields of corn and soybeans, to the loneliness of tree rows left standing as boundaries and windbreaks. The characters in *Criminal Tendencies* are transients and I thought of one or two coming from this area, with these memories in their heads. A vividly painted van that a character drives in the novel is the vehicle of a man who lives on a county road I often traveled on my way into Elkhart.

There are other sights I will always identify as Indianian, since I saw them, or noticed them, or associated them first with Indiana, like the ubiquitous, portable yellow sign or billboard, its top edge often arrow shaped, usually surrounded with an edging of illumination.

Highway 80, the "Main Street of America" as it boasts itself to be, I travel quite frequently; it is indeed a symbolic artery. The town of Gary, its various mills, is redolent with symbolism, too, as well as its own history of odors. I spent a day going through the Bethlehem Steel Mill at Burns Harbor, Indiana, an experience, I trust, that won't be spared chronicling by me in fiction. Every day the bounty of place stands revealed, often in unexpected ways, announcing improbable portents: Pickup trucks with oversized tires, which I take to be testicular, swollen images of exaggerated masculinity. But these things are incremental, for a place does seep into you, as well as settle over you. Questions revolving around the literature of place often come down to this: does the place claim you? Do you claim the place?

When I think of where I live, this topmost part of Indiana, its northern most reach, I picture the whole state as a full water glass, a tumbler, which its shape does somewhat resemble. Into that glass someone has poured a powdery substance and has stirred it up. It has begun to settle: that is my image of where I live. Whatever I think Indiana is, whatever mysterious substances, unknowable essences, make up its mix, the thickest part of it gathers at the bottom of the state, the middle is cloudy, but not as dense, and at the top, where I live, it is almost clear, though not quite.

❦ Michael Schelle

IMPULSIVE INDIANA INSPIRATION

UPON COMPLETION of this essay I realized that my prose is similar to my musical compositions: elements of contradiction, kaleidescopic approaches, anger, and frenzy—some experimental language for good measure—coexist with certain moments of relaxation, intimacy, tenderness, and optimism.

A writer's handbook I consulted mentioned that "anyone who wishes to become a good writer should endeavor, before being tempted by the more showy qualities, to be direct, simple, brief and lucid." Well, this lets out my essay and, unfortunately, most of my favorite writers and composers!

Nevertheless, in the name of directness and simplicity (not to mention lucidity), I have organized this piece into four movements. As a composer, I find these subsections from within to be extremely helpful when trying to control my otherwise schizophrenic and eclectic materials.

Movement I: Images of Indiana and the Hoosier Experience

Let us address here the first impression of Hoosierism. The Indiana experience must mean something to *us*. It's our home, our base of creative operations. Yet, Indiana's image across the country is, we often say, dominated by seed corn caps and basketballs. Indiana is changing; nevertheless, an artistic image and tradition is still far from what we're famous for. Perhaps we maintain, and actually cultivate, our less than cosmopolitan artistic image by too often acknowledging only James Whitcomb Riley, Booth Tarkington, Hoagy Carmichael, John Cougar Mellencamp, and Garfield. All are noteworthy but do we promote them at the expense of the more radical Kurt Vonnegut, Theodore Dreiser, Ned Rorem, and Ezra Pound? These latter artists aren't really denied or ignored, but rather left on their own without much Indiana support. Sometimes we act like our own worst enemies . . . and each time an artist "gives up" on Indiana a negative image is reaffirmed.

I like the reference to Ezra Pound. After receiving degrees in literature at Hamilton College and the University of Pennsylvania, Pound, in 1907, accepted a teaching position at Wabash College in Crawfordsville, as Professor of Romance Languages.

The story has it that, although the Father of Imagism claimed total innocence, he was fired from his position in a few short months because of alleged wrongdoings with the local ladies. This charge summed up, for Pound, all of the vice that pervaded the world he named "Devil's Island, Indiana."This may be one of the earliest examples of bad press for aesthetic Indiana. Yet Pound's shortlived brush with the Indiana experience apparently haunted him for the rest of his life; some critics seized upon this Hoosier episode as a partial explanation for Pound's many years as an expatriate and anti-Midwesterner.

Since my move to Indiana in 1979, Pound has been of particular interest as an influence in my work. Always a fan of the experimental, American poetry in general, the Philadelphia connection (my birthplace), and, last but not least, my curiosity about the concept of insanity versus genius (besides Pound, Strindberg, Poe, and Kafka—none of whom were offered jobs in Indiana), I have found this ex-Hoosier to be a great inspiration. In addition, Pound loved contemporary music—he was an enthusiast for Bartok, Stravinsky, and the early twentieth century experimentalists. In the 1930s, Pound saved priceless Vivaldi manuscripts from bombs and artillery fire, demanding of local officials that they be microfilmed (then a new and rare procedure) for safekeeping. Later, during an invasion, these original manuscripts were destroyed and today musicians are performing from copies made from Pound's microfilms.

What a marvelous experience Pound's Devil's Island, Indiana turned out to be. In 1914, in the underground magazine *Blast*, Pound wrote: "Blast first England. Curse its climate for its sins and infections. Dismal symbol, set round our bodies, of effeminate lout within. . . . " Some critics believe that, between the lines, Pound is actually blasting America and, specifically, the Midwest mentality.

Well, if this is the image we must survive and, ultimately, reverse, the best way is to use our own, more positive artists to spread the optimistic word about Indiana. If the artistic environment here is on the negative side, why do we maintain a strong cross-section of talented painters, writers, dancers, composers, and thinkers? For most of us it probably comes down to practical, economic and domestic situations. But, for a few, there is also the distinct challenge of trying to develop a positive national profile while based in In-diana.

Our state seal displays a buffalo, a farmer, and a mountain. Which is the part that's misleading? Although we are certainly dealing with some notion of tradition, is this a fair representation of our considerable diversity?

Movement II: Scherzo: Aesthetic Taste, Perception, and Decision Making

Musical scherzos are usually quite brief, to the point, and often somewhat tongue-in-cheek. How a listener might react to a musical scherzo depends on many factors including environment, ancestry, upbringing, and peer pressure. A crucial element of our perceptive abilities is connected to taste. It is this factor that can, sometimes unfairly, make or break an artist or artistic environment.

A lot in Indiana depends on taste. Bertolt Brecht once said: "There are times when you have to choose between being human and having taste." Most of us have already made up our minds about what we do and do not like. Regardless of background and intellect, too often it's that "gut feeling" that determines our perception and decision making process.

The Indiana artist is continually bombarded with a cross-section of popular taste, political taste, abstract, professional, and personal taste. The most difficult task of any work is to grab our attention and then hold us to discover the skeleton beneath the flesh. There will always be those artists who, in seeking success and acceptance, will try to cater to a variety of tastes. My own personal aesthetic is actually rather simple: I have to love it first . . . if I love it chances are my enthusiasm will be infectious, perhaps even encourage some listeners to pull away from their preconceived "taste environments" in an honest attempt to expand their horizons.

As Indiana artists, is one of our jobs to help develop and evolve taste (and, consequently, perception, understanding, and comprehension)? To help people go beyond taste and immediate reactions and toward a more unified, personal and thorough approach to experience? As the Princeton composer, Milton Babbitt, once said in a now infamous article from the 1960s: "Who Cares if You Listen?"

IN 1981 RESEARCHERS AT INDIANA UNIVERSITY DISCOVERED THAT DISCO MUSIC CAUSES HOMOSEXUALITY IN PIGS AND DEAFNESS IN RATS!

Our own personal tastes and perceptions of this report will cause us to react in a variety of ways. Some will laugh, some snicker under their breath, some will become flushed, some will question the inclusion of such a statement in this essay (!), some will seriously proclaim, ''I knew it!'' or in all innocence ask, ''It does?''—and if you love disco music you will be personally offended. What we all share upon being confronted by this proclamation is curiosity.

Curiosity has its own reason for existing and existence, alone, can help generate change in the arts and humanities. In nature, in the laws of physics and magnetism, and in our everyday experience we see opposites attracting— but only if the poles are extreme. Hems go up this year because they went down last year. We might have global problems in order to find global solutions. Decay fosters growth. As John Cage points out in the world of experimental music: ''We had to conceive of silence in order to open our ears.''

Movement III: Adagio: Personal Impulsive Indiana Inspiration

If there is such an ism as Hoosierism, it has greatly contributed to my personal inspiration. It is said that you can't explain (therefore define) inspiration—it just happens. But, let's say, for me inspiration is: ''A reaction or response to an experience (person/place/thing).''

I suspect that most of us do not derive inspiration from the old romantic standbys—strolling through the woods, watching an ocean sunset, perceiving the majesty of a mountain, etc., etc. I know these things have never really worked for me and, since I've lived in Indianapolis for nearly ten years, it's lucky I don't have to rely on natural wonders for my impulsive inspiration.

I find my strongest inspiration in everyday matter—people, places, and experiences that might seem commonplace to most but actually can and do generate exciting and, sometimes, unique ideas. I have found my Indiana inspiration at the Castleton Mall, the State Fair, the Indy 500 and, in more personal ways, through contact with Indiana people. Indirectly, I have discovered a kind of generic inspiration from the Indiana image already mentioned.

I love my work and, for the most part, the results—my style, my isms. Not that my work is meant to represent Hoosierisms in the last part of the twentieth century; simply put, it is right for me. As a result, my outlook on the state of the artistic state may be slanted toward optimism.

Movement IV: Finale, Recapitulation, and "In Conclusion"

We might begin this movement with the thought that artists are an impractical yet luxurious commodity (or accessory) for the chosen few of breeding and class. It is interesting: I think that almost without exception, academic and arts organizations will count among their Board members the respected giants of industry, medicine, and business. But I have yet to see one composer, one philosopher, one poet on the Board of a local bank or insurance company.

Artists look at things differently, yet we must survive and succeed in the world of practicalities. We are, the practical man believes, dreamers, the unrealistic ones, even antagonists and escapists. Artificial lines are drawn discouraging the way into fresh experience represented by impulsive creativity. Although the Indiana environment has greatly improved during my stay here (there really are more honest attempts to recognize our state's natural artistic resources) circumspection seems called for. Unchecked or poorly nurtured growth could lead to two dangerous isms: dilletantism and amateurism—and ultimately to an ultra-conservative base for the state's artistic product.

There are many reasons why the cutting edge artist finds trouble in experiencing Indiana yet it is this very trouble that can launch us into the twenty-first century. Reaction has long been a terrific inspirational force for writers and, in place of grumbling about the Hoosier cultural climate, perhaps we can make it work for us. Practical art will always fulfill a need, but original creative art can create a need.

I believe the 1990s are an exciting threshold for Indiana. Our national image is improving on many fronts; Indianapolis is considered one of America's most livable cities. But Indiana's direction should avoid slick industrial and domestic packaging. It's already too difficult for the public to tell the wood from the veneer. Microwave chicken recipes have what they call "browning chemicals" to make the bird look like it was roasted in your good old-fashioned convection oven. We have disposable diapers, disposable cameras, disposable people, and disposable morals. We live in an age where our product taste and many of our concepts and decisions are controlled or, rather, formulated.

Many people view our time as an age of contradictions—the end of a unique Western Civilization. We are told not to engage in casual sex yet we're bombarded with sex from morning til night on everything from MTV to catfood commercials. It is hard to discern the commercially formulated product from the authentic; the produced from the productive; groupthink from individual thought. Too often, we don't seem to mind.

In the modern arts, a few people seem to decide our taste for us. Some rock and rollers are convinced there is a thirteen-year-old girl named Tiffany somewhere in New York City who makes all the corporate choices for major recording companies. More than ever, certain isms in writing, music and painting are "hot" or "in" at the expense of worthwhile alternatives.

This is dangerous from the standpoint of creative legacy—be it Indiana or national. Some artists, in their desire for solid acceptance and success in their chosen field, dispose of their original track in favor of the bandwagon of instantaneous gratification. Disposable aesthetics come next.

A few months ago my little boy had to undergo some rather tricky surgery. As I sat in the waiting room for several hours, aside from being "artistically inspired" by the experience, I was thinking about many things. Practical things, aesthetic things, religious things, domestic things. In thinking about my son, for some reason, it occurred to me that he would be graduating from high school in the year 2001. What would music be like then . . . what will my music be like then? Will Nutrasweet . . . and Dan Quayle . . . still be around?

For whatever reason, my wondering turned sour—to a more pragmatic and, yes, practical career discouragement as I recalled the commercialization of the wonderful Strauss score "Thus Spake Zarathustra" in the 1969 film *2001: A Space Odyssey*.

My anxiety, anticipation, and concern for the surgery at hand prompted more examples to pop into mind, stirring yet more anger, anxiety, and hostility . . . Ravel's "Bolero" in the movie *10*; Mozart in *Elvira Madigan*;

Bach fugues to sell Timex watches. Now, tiny excerpts, fragments actually, of the glorious Mozart Requiem are selling Levis with my favorite six measures of the "Lacrymosa" accompanying the supple young coed bending over in her tight, stonewashed denims.

We often complain that Indiana is viewed as a butt for this advertising approach—we're a little unsuspecting, a little naive and behind the times. We're not quite as slick as the other "apolises," coastal cities and nationally recognized centers for whatever. Even if this were the case, and if jaded New Yorkers were the preferred way to go in dealing with our fellow artists and colleagues, perhaps we could capitalize on this very problem and show the rest of the country what is really real: we might share with the coasts that think they have the answers to Nietzsche's dictum: "All truth is simple and that is a lie."

We might show the rest of the country that our homespun Hoosier ideals (of which we are so often accused) might actually provide the ammunition needed to backlash our accusers. Here, in Indiana, we might use our own style of sophistication to fight the dehumanization of heart and mind with solid artistic and practical values that honestly carry the species into the future—into the truth.

❦ Hal Higdon

INDIANA SPORTS

ONE LABOR Day at the Blueberry Festival in Plymouth, Indiana, a friend asked: "Do you plan to participate in the Crap Shoot?"

"I never play dice," I responded.

"You don't understand what a Crap Shoot means." My friend explained that for one dollar I could choose a plot of ground in a nearby pasture. Others did the same. Then organizers released a cow. On whichever plot the cow deposited its next cow pie determined the winner of $500.

I opined that that had to be the low point of sports in Indiana. The high point? Most people might choose basketball, although certainly a case could be made for the Indy 500. Or various Olympic sports from track and field to bicycling. Or football with the Colts now in Indianapolis and Notre Dame winning national championships again in South Bend.

But others might rank all of those sports on the same level with the Crap Shoot. Is sports in Indiana, particularly basketball, overemphasized? When the president of the state's largest university apologizes in public to keep his basketball coach from moving to New Mexico, one would think so. Several years ago, I traveled through rural Indiana, stopping frequently in general stores and cafes. In most other states, you would see calendar pinups of naked women on the wall; in Indiana, it's Bobby Knight.

Nobody can deny basketball's magic appeal in Indiana. In the movie *Hoosiers*, the coach played by Gene Hackman says, "My boys only know basketball, farming, and school—probably in that order." The Hackman film chronicled the victory of a rural school with sixty-four students that miraculously (with the help of a good outside shooter) wins the state title. It was based, loosely, on the tiny town of Milan's having won the title in 1954.

Most people outside Indiana know about "Hoosier Hysteria," centered each February on the state high school basketball tournament. I've always considered that tournament, stretching over four weekends, cruel. Since each of Indiana's 388 schools participates, that guarantees that all but one ends its season on a losing note. In all but one community, Monday morning's papers feature photographs of cheerleaders crying.

Yet Hoosiers probably are no more sports mad than fans in other states. And lately they have an increasing variety of sports—participant as well as spectator—from which to choose. Nevertheless, for large parts of Indiana, Gene Hackman's film quote remains quite true.

I moved to Indiana in 1964. My wife and I were born and raised in Chicago, but wanted to escape hectic urban life. As a runner, I also longed to live where I could run through the open countryside, rather than down city streets. We chose Michigan City, community of 38,000 in northwestern Indiana, because it seemed like a decent place to raise a family. It never occurred to us that the move might confer on us—and our children—the label "Hoosiers."

Today, after a quarter century in Indiana, I'm still not sure I identify with that label. Chicago remains only an hour's drive away, compared to three hours for Indianapolis. Living and working on Lake Michigan, I can look from my office (at least on clear days) and see the tips of Chicago skyscrapers. I still view Chicago TV channels, read Chicago newspapers, and attend concerts of the Chicago Symphony Orchestra and games of the Chicago Cubs, Bears, and Bulls. At times, I have been hard pressed to remember the names of Indiana's governor and U.S. senators.

I first realized I was in Indiana during a conversation about basketball with a neighbor my first winter in town. The neighbor's description of the mania at high school games intrigued me. I volunteered to attend one: "Let me know next time you're going, and I'll come along."

He laughed and explained—politely—that one did not commit to a single game in Indiana, you committed to a *season*. You could not get in the door unless you had a season ticket. And you could not obtain a season ticket unless you appeared one night in November, along with about twice as many people as would fit into the high school's merely 3,950-seat gymnasium, and had your name drawn by lottery. Indeed, this was my first indication that basketball in Indiana was akin to a Crap Shoot.

Thus, before the 1965–66 season, my wife and I trekked to the high school gym, not caring that much whether we won or lost, but interested in playing the game. We sat more amused than nervous as the school principal, dressed in a garish red sports jacket (the school colors were red and white), rotated a circular cage containing the names of individuals desiring season tickets. When he announced the names of those winning the right to purchase those tickets, people actually applauded. Among the names drawn that evening were ours.

And so, almost against our will, we became high school basketball fans. The school's official name was Elston High School, but its players wore the pointedly simple name "City" on their jerseys. They were nicknamed the "Red Devils," and the head cheerleader among seven wore a Devil's costume, complete with pitchfork with which to threaten opposing teams. The packed gym echoed to the frantic screams of the fans, orchestrated by those cheerleaders, as City annihilated its opponents, schools from other nearby towns like Elkhart, South Bend, and LaPorte. Scores were embarrassingly lopsided. At the beginning of the year, I cheered secretly for the other teams to at least keep the games close and therefore interesting. Of course, by the end of the season, I had become infected with Hoosier Hysteria to the point where I too was screaming shamelessly at each City basket and booing should the referee dare call a foul on one of our innocent players. Even a margin of 20 points was insufficient to whet my lust.

So at the end of the season, City traveled downstate to the same gymnasium on the campus of Butler University pictured in the Gene Hackman movie and won the state title.

I don't believe I appreciated, at the time, the significance of that victory, or comprehended my luck in having moved into town just in time to obtain season tickets to City's first—and to this date only—state basketball title. Only as the years have passed have I begun to realize what I, in a small way, was part of.

Echoes of the state title year remain. Larger than life-size cutout photos of the dozen players on the 1965–66 team remain attached to one wall in the high school gym. But that gym rarely is filled any more, no more lotteries being necessary. Addition of a second high school in town diluted both the talent and fan interest. Every now and then I see one of the players from the championship season, middle-aged now, at a local lumber yard or car dealership. My wife and I continued to attend games during our children's high school years. Our daughter was a cheerleader. After she graduated, we gradually lost interest.

Although Hoosier Hysteria still remains, I sense a similar lessening of interest in high school basketball throughout the state. Some suggest the consolidation of schools in rural areas, eliminating old rivalries, has conspired to dampen the fires of enthusiasm. That may be true, but the increasing popularity of the college game is another factor. Bobby Knight's frequent trips with his Indiana team to the NCAA's "Final Four" (including national championships in 1976, 1981, and 1987) has caused the state high school tournament to seem, well, minor league. Purdue and Notre Dame also field top-ranked basketball teams. The Indiana Pacers play in the National Basketball Association, though they never have ascended to the top of that league or elicited much fan support.

The same is true with the Indianapolis (once Baltimore) Colts of the National Football League. The Colts are imported, not homegrown; the legacy of Johnny Unitas did not translate well. When the Chicago Bears visited at the start of the 1988 season, a record crowd of over 60,000 appeared at the Hoosier Dome, many of them come to cheer the Bears rather than the Colts. After the home town lost by less than a touchdown, one local TV reporter rationalized the defeat away: "At least the Bears won."

Meanwhile in baseball, although the Chamber of Commerce would love to lure a major league franchise to Indianapolis, most Hoosiers seem content to support the Reds in Cincinnati or the Cubs and White Sox in Chicago. Why not? Look at all the people living outside Indiana who cheer, cheer for Old Notre Dame. Also, autoracing fans throughout the world look to the state as home of the Indianapolis 500.

The Indy 500 actually dwarfs high school basketball in its mass appeal. "You don't plan anything in this city, whether an opera or a dinner party, without first checking the 500 schedule," says one Indianapolis resident. In addition to the auto race, the month-long 500 Festival includes dances, break-fasts, parties for children, a 13-mile running race, and a two-hour parade viewed by 500,000 along its route and by 25 million on TV.

I've participated in the running race, billed as the 500 Festival Mini-Marathon, actually 13.1 miles long, starting in downtown Indianapolis at Monument Circle and finishing on the Speedway track. The "Mini" (as it is called) is barely known outside state borders, 98 percent of entrants coming from Indiana, 80 percent from Indianapolis and environs. Limited to 7,500, you must file your entry within three weeks of when blanks are distributed, otherwise you wait until next year. It took me three years of trying before I figured out the system and gained entry.

All that, of course, serves merely as *antipasto* for the main course on the Sunday of Memorial Day weekend: the auto race. The Indianapolis Motor Speedway is privately owned by the family of the late Tony Hulman, thus its officials always have been reluctant to discuss numbers, whether dollars or even seats surrounding the massive 2.5-mile oval track. The Speedway brochure claims 235,000 seats, but a reporter for the Indianapolis *Star* once was assigned by that paper to count the actual number of those seats. He determined the number as 255,702. They sell for between $18 and $90, the high-priced seats being so valuable that heirs to estates and parties to divorces fight over them. Add to that number those who pay $15 to stand in the infield and the one-day attendance probably approaches half a million, the take, conservatively, $20 million, not including hot dogs and beer. Given those figures, you can hardly quarrel with the 500's billing itself as "the greatest spectacle in racing."

Perhaps the single most riveting moment in sport occurs each year after the balloons go up and TV star Jim Nabors sings "Back Home Again in Indiana." The pace car that has escorted the starting field two laps around the track suddenly darts into the pits, leaving 33 gleaming racing machines to battle for position going into the first turn. A half million spectators collectively hold their breath.

As a reporter, I've watched the race from the pits and from the grandstand, but remember most vividly sitting with my family in 1973 atop the knoll within the infield between Turns One and Two. (That knoll now has been preempted by the Speedway Museum.) We heard the rising roar as the cars, unseen by us because of grandstands in the way, accelerated. But then the roar died, and only a few cars came through the turn, moving slowly. I looked back toward the main straightaway and saw a column of dark smoke rising over the grandstands. Something horrible had happened, but many minutes passed before the crowd learned that a third of the cars had crashed, and although nobody was killed, a driver and mechanic would die in the race after it had been restarted.

In contrast, track and field seems almost a subdued sport, the speeds a mere tenth of those in auto racing and without the specter of death waiting at the end of the straightaway. Yet, I'll remember just as vividly the long jump competition at the 1988 Olympic Trials that pitted 1984 gold medalist Carl Lewis against Larry Myricks, an excellent jumper, who nevertheless had lost to Lewis in 33 consecutive competitions since 1981.

In Indianapolis, Myricks exploded with a jump over 28 feet. On his second jump, Lewis waited at the end of the runway waiting for officials to rake the pit. A hush fell over the crowd, every eye on Lewis. And in that moment of expectation, the heavens opened. A drenching rainstorm hit.

Lewis, certain to qualify for one of the three positions on the Olympic team in that event, could have passed or asked officials for a delay. But Lewis probably still remembered the criticism from the press in 1984 when, in winning the gold medal, he took only two jumps and passed the rest. He didn't want to disappoint the people in the cheap seats again—or maybe he didn't want to disappoint himself.

So even as spectators fumbled for umbrellas or scrambled for shelter under the stands, Lewis began to run, arms pumping, legs lifting, his characteristic straight-backed sprint. As rain pelted him, he hit the board and lifted into space, not to descend to earth until he had soared exactly two inches beyond the jump by Myricks.

Lewis stood, looked briefly down at the crater he had just made in the sand, and turned to the wildly applauding crowd and raised his palms as though to say: No sweat.

The rain eventually stopped, and both Myricks and Lewis continued to improve their jumps, Lewis edging the other jumper by less than an inch. But it was Carl Lewis's jump in the rain that will remain etched in my mind as I remember great moments in Indiana sport.

It is easy to get upset about the excesses of sport: cheating, drugs, violence, bad manners among both spectators and participants, the huge sums offered athletes while policemen and teachers go underpaid. That the media devote excessive time, effort, and space to covering sports seems, well . . . I am reminded once more of the Crap Shoot.

Still, though 388 basketball teams embark on the road to victory each February in Indiana and only one emerges joyously triumphant, it becomes a victory for us all, just as tiny Milan's win in 1954 remains more than three decades later a symbol of hope and youthful achievement that even Hollywood hype can't taint. The tears of the cheerleaders crying for their losing teams are as quickly forgotten as they are quickly shed. We identify with the winners.

Many of us in life suffer defeats, and others experience victories, but often such defeats and victories are not only fleeting, they are ambiguous; you can't tell for certain whether you won or lost. In sports there is never any doubt. Someone emerges. It goes into the record books. You can look it up decades later.

I had come to Plymouth, Indiana, that Labor Day not for the Crap Shoot, but rather to run the Blueberry Stomp, a 15-kilometer race that attracts more than a thousand runners each year. Part of the attraction is that the race starts down Plymouth's Michigan Avenue just before the Blueberry Festival parade, reportedly one of the biggest parades in Indiana. People begin gathering hours before the parade to claim the best viewing areas, so runners who normally run and race unseen and uncheered can experience the excitement of running before a crowd estimated at 75,000.

The day was cool for September; clouds shaded us from the sun. I positioned myself near the front so that when the cannon sounded signaling the race start, I would not be delayed by slower runners. I was off fast and was only peripherally aware that I was running past those awaiting the parade.

Soon we turned off the main street, passed a cemetery on the edge of town, and found ourselves running down a rural road shaded by trees on both sides. We dipped downward as the road passed over a creek bed, ascended, then dipped again. We passed farmhouses and corn fields so typical of this area of middle America. Still focused on my own performance, I was barely aware of this postcard scene or the other runners around me, all waging their own internal battles. We looped back, and runners returning occupied one half of the road, slower runners still going out, the other. Several called me by name, and I tried to respond.

In the final mile, we returned to the parade route, moving against the grain of floats carrying beauty queens and Shriners circling on miniature motorcycles. Someone on a float threw candy to the crowd, and I had to dodge around a little girl who leaped out into the street to claim some. I thought she was in the way, and she probably thought I was in the way.

It occurred to me that few in the crowd were devoting much attention to the finishing runners now that the parade occupied the same route. We were merely background; focus had shifted away from sports.

And certainly that is how it should be in Indiana and elsewhere. Sports are an important diversion, but should be considered only that: part of the background of real life regardless of what the Gene Hackman character said in the movie. As I neared the end of the Blueberry Stomp, I realized that I was finishing in the top 50, not bad for an old man, so approaching the line I raised my arms as a signal of my personal victory. And on the last stride, a younger runner ducked under one outstretched arm and caused me to finish 51st. I laughed. No cheerleaders cried.

I had participated in the Crap Shoot after all.

🍂 James Alexander Thom

ON BEING AN OLD STUMP

AS EVERYONE knows, Indiana is divided into two parts:

1. Basketball.
2. All That Other Stuff.

At the risk of losing all my Hoosier readers at once, I am going to ignore Number 1 and go to All That Other Stuff. One reason is that here on the ridge where I chose to build my house, there isn't any ground level enough to dribble on. If I shot a basketball into the air, it would hit a redbud or a redbird, an oak or an owl, a hickory or a hummingbird. If I shouted a cheer for Bobby Knight, I would scare the deer that go down in the twilight to drink at the pond.

Any Hoosier might well ask me, "Why in the world did you choose to build a house on a place too steep for dribbling, or too wooded for a clear shot at a backboard?"

The reason goes back a long way, back to a fork in the road in my formative years nearly half a century ago, when I took the road less traveled by, and the basketball folks all trooped down the other, dribbling and whooping. My parents, both young Hoosier-born Indiana University Medical school graduates fresh out of their internships, found the tiny town of Gosport to set up practice. (That's medical practice, not basketball practice.) Gosport is a river town in Owen County, a part of Southern Indiana Uplands. In the best of times, Owen County is hardscrabble country, and my parents arrived during the Great Depression. Folks couldn't afford to go to doctors much. Most of them knew how to take care of themselves if they did get sick or hurt. If they couldn't cure it themselves they'd just tough it out as long as they could. Mother tells of an old farm woman who had appendicitis, which developed into peritonitis. By the time she finally let someone summon the doctor, she was bent double. And since she was already stooped over, she was picking strawberries when Mother arrived. I was born in a bedroom upstairs from the doctors' office waiting room, which was usually empty.

My mother took turns delivering other people's babies and having her own four. She resourcefully combined her professional career with motherhood, long before the question arose about whether that was possible. When she had house calls to make out in the country, she put us in the back seat of the old black sedan with a picnic basket, and we would go with her on her rounds of those paint-peeling farmhouses in the hollows and along the dusty roads. The barefooted kids on those pig-trampled, chicken-squawking farmsteads had too many chores to do much dribbling or basket-shooting, and couldn't afford basketballs anyway. Still, many of them dreamed basketball. I never did. I was more captivated by the arrowheads the plows turned up in bottomlands. I ran the ridges not in basketball sneakers but homemade moccasins and leggings. My pals and I were aware that Indiana meant "Land of the Indians," and the Bears of Blue River prowled and growled in our dreams.

On the way home from her round of house calls then, Mother—"Doc Julia," as she was known—would stop at some overlook along a ridge road. She had an eye for great views and enchanted meadows. And there we would have a picnic amid the wildflowers or ferns, with a distant rank of hazy-blue ridgelines making our horizon.

Thus, almost by osmosis, these hardy hill people and their landscape began to be a part of me, even before I gave a thought to how remarkable they were.

In particular, there was a household of ancient Quakers, who lived in a sway-backed, vine-covered old pioneer cottage on a backbone ridge in the southeastern part of the county. They were almost penniless, but their way of life was rich, serene, and in harmony with the countryside. They raised almost everything they ate, they had a cow for milk, cheese, and butter, they sold eggs for kitchen money, they wove on a massive handmade loom, and made much of their own clothing. They obtained sweet water from a dug well under a cool, vine-shaded wellhouse, letting guest children crank the wooden winch to bring up the pail, and drink it from gourd dippers. They had no plumbing, no electricity, no radio, and made their own entertainment by reciting verse or singing around a foot-pumped organ in the parlor. Sometimes the neighbor boys would bring their guitars and fiddles up to add to the volume. The old widow Etta Macey, guiding spirit of the household, had advice for any guests who might be too accustomed to modern conveniences. "If thee needs anything and cannot find it, come to me and I'll tell thee how to get along without it," she would say with a chuckle. That, too, soaked into my soul and stayed there.

In the evenings, Etta would lead guests to a place down the road, a place that overlooked a ten-mile vista of hills and valleys darkening under the sunset, and we would watch until the last tinge of rose faded out of the dusk. Etta would philosophize with reverence and humor. Then we would walk back up to her little house and light the coal-oil lamps and the fireplace. Although I did not consciously decide that I would someday build a house on this high, steep, wooded spot, the seed of the notion was planted, just as surely as were the wild woods flowers those old Quakers transplanted around their yard more than half a century ago—wildflowers that still abound where that old house used to be.

My next forty years were a sort of odyssey, to good places and bad, through war and peace, ambition and despair, love and rejection, all the things that lives are made of.

As a little boy I saw the Indiana countryside from the windows of great New York Central passenger trains pulled by steam locomotives driven by my own grandfather. As a big boy I boarded just such a train in the echoing Union Station to go to war in a place called Korea, which I had scarcely heard of before. As a student and journalist I watched Indianapolis grow from a coalsmoke-gray, trolley-wired city rooted in the nineteenth century to a high-tech metropolis self-conscious about its new arts centers and sports arenas. The more I moved among the city's powerful and saw how they controlled or retarded the city's development, the more I thought about the hardy, droll, unpresuming folk I had known in rural Owen County's hills. With every city my journalistic career took me to, with every cynical lesson I learned in a dirty, teeming, frantic world, I felt more strongly the pull of this backbone ridge in Owen County and its hazy sunsets. When I would return to these hills to visit my mother, I would come up to this place above the valley every evening, sit with a pipe and a walking stick, and watch the sun go down. The view never changed, except that the old Quakers weren't here anymore— not in body, I should say. Though most of my favorite places in America were being built over and covered with industrial waste and garish commercial architecture, this long valley year after year escaped ruination. It became a sort of haven from progress; perhaps thinking like a red man, I never could see the white man's "progress" as much of a boon.

In my mid-forties, as a magazine writer living in a Chicago condominium and having to pass through three security systems just to get to the outdoors (which was paved), I sold the *National Geographic* on the idea of a story about the Southern Indiana Uplands and the self-reliant people who lived there. The assignment was a labor of love and a good excuse to turn my back on the haste and waste of Chicago for a while.

For weeks then I rambled in those beloved uplands and became reacquainted with the sort of folks I had known. In Chicago I had hardly ever heard a conversation about anything besides prices, fashions, schemes, or crooked politicians; here in the hills I could learn of things good and useful almost any time anyone opened his mouth. A favorite kind of talk among these people is about the ways of doing things well, and it is valuable talk because of all the experience behind it.

The interviewing was a joy, and warm friendships grew out of it. And if I was anywhere near this ridge in eastern Owen County when the sun began to go down, I came up here and smoked and gazed, calm at heart.

I had a chance to take a job any magazine writer would covet, one that would move me to Washington, D. C., and I would ponder it up here on this ridge.

By the time the story was done, I knew I could not return to Chicago, or go to Washington or any other city. The circle had rolled around; the odyssey was over; it was time to put my roots down on the ridge and build my final home above the sunset valley.

Escaping from the modern world and landing on this old limestone ridge was something like parachuting from a jet plane and trying to land on the saddle of a waiting horse. But I landed right and the moment I was on the ridge, things began to go my way. Books I had been writing without success for fifteen years began to find publishers. A little money began to trickle in so I could pay off the debts of my mis-adventures in the cities. And so at the age of fifty I moved into a tent on the ridge and started clearing brush for a house site. My sister, knowing I wanted to build a log house, kept her eyes open and found a 150-year-old hewn-poplar log structure that an old widow wanted torn down so she would no longer have to pay taxes on it. This I disassembled and moved to my ridge-top site and started rebuilding it with my own inexperienced but eager hands. As I moved these massive logs into place, I admired the precise dovetail joints that long-ago craftsmen had made with their crude tools, and felt that I was continuing work started when Indiana was a new state. The hill Hoosiers I so admired were mostly descended from the kind of people who had hewed and hoisted these great logs; Scotch-Irish pioneers arriving in the Indiana uplands by way of Kentucky and Virginia. My own ancestors had come that way from Scotland in 1740 and the decades following. It seemed natural for me to be here on a wooded Indiana ridge felling trees and hewing timbers—anachronistic, perhaps, but certainly more natural than opening condominium doors by pushbutton code in Chicago.

I could see that this housebuilding would call for the kind of strength, durability, and resourcefulness that I had admired in my fellow hill-dwellers, and I could only hope that I would meet the test.

The nature of Southern Indiana's terrain and weather, of course, made the test as grueling as anyone could have predicted. Rain, wind, mud, heat and cold, sleet and mold: for two years these rampaged through my building site, always at the worst times, causing warpage, leaks, heat exhaustion, injuries, and frustration. Trees, steepness, and stone made this the spectacular site I had so wanted, but they compounded the difficulty of the building task. Everywhere I needed to dig there were roots and bedrock. Trucks could not come in through the steep woods; logs and building stones had to be carried or snaked in by muscle and primitive engineering devices. The log-raising was done by block and tackle, with just me on the end of the rope; I hadn't enough money then to hire any help. I have always tackled big projects with a fool's optimism, but never had I strained and labored like this to finish them.

But uplanders live by the philosophy that the worthwhile things don't come easy, and this test confirmed my notion that I am an uplander and nothing else. Now this house, all native poplar and oak and elm, logs and posts and beams and local sandstone, stands here on the ridge among the tall hardwoods just as I had envisioned it in my dreams for forty years, and it looks as if it had grown here. Every heavy log and sill and stone in it I have shaped, dragged or hoisted, and all that lifting has rooted me more firmly on this piece of ground, as if it had driven my feet into the soil.

And there is an additional benefit. Now when I write my books about the pioneers in this territory, I know their tools and materials and methods intimately, and know just how it feels to use them. Call it another form of research.

The odyssey is over and the dream is fulfilled. I look out and see miles of unpeopled Indiana hill scenery in every direction, and I can watch the sunset beyond the valley, and I can still feel the spirits of the hardy old

Quakers around me, and, farther back but no more remote, the spirits of the Indians whose hunting camps were in the creek bottoms. In the meadows far below, my horses graze and amble, as theirs did. The seasons turn. I grow older in a steady hush of passing time, but I don't feel it. There are projects enough to keep me busy till I'm a hundred, and I feel the strength coming up into me from the clay and limestone, coming down into me from the hazy light. That feeling is the spirit of place. A stony ridge is like the backbone of a horse, and on this ridge I feel as if I were being carried onward toward the comprehension of the important meanings. Deep below, I feel, is the heart of my country. Everywhere else I have felt as if I were on an outer rim, away from the center of the world.

"Oh, you're from Indiana?" people say when I travel. "Great basketball out there! Big Red!" To many, that's the spirit of my home country. But to me the spirit of the place is something that was here long before basketball was invented. Like the red men whose land this was, I don't want to leave it. You'd have to pry me out of it the way I've budged out the roots and boulders where my house stands. I keep a wary eye to the future, and work and hope for the best, but what I really am is an old stump, still vital; I still sprout in the changing world, but my roots are old and deep.

❦ James H. Madison

LOOKING BACKWARD

Transitions and Traditions in Indiana

HOOSIERS LIVE in a time of transition. As the twentieth century wanes, the sense grows that the old order is giving way to the new. All about us are signs of change, signs often seen through a gloomy haze. Where are we going, Hoosiers want to know. Are we in the midst of a sea change, a radical shift in the way we live, an upheaval that will require abandonment of our traditions?

No sensible historian will answer such questions with confidence; few historians, recognizing the complexities of understanding the past, will venture even to speak about the present. Yet the student of Indiana's past knows a simple but often ignored truth that may be of value in facing present and future: this is not the first generation of Hoosiers to live in a time of transition. Hoosiers have often faced uncertain futures. "The times they are a-changing," the great anthem of the 1960s proclaimed, but it could have been sung by each preceding generation (though to a different beat and tune).

Three eras stand out in Indiana's past as times of crisis and change, as times when the future seemed most uncertain and the prophets of doom gained large audiences. The conflict of Civil War, the late–nineteenth century era of industrialization, and the stirring reform promised by the New Deal brought frightening clashes of thunder and lightning to the Indiana landscape. Each portended a revolutionary shift in the lives of Hoosiers, a radical departure. Yet, in fact, and with the advantage of the historian's hindsight, it is possible to argue that each of these apparent breaks from tradition proved less than revolutionary. In each period Hoosiers built on earlier traditions, seeking bridges to new eras, different, to be sure, but not radical departures from what went before.

The Civil War tested the mettle of all Americans. For Indiana the challenge was especially poignant. Would Hoosiers, many with family ties to the South, dress in blue or gray at the nation's most dangerous moment? Would the body politic, threatened by potentially disloyal Copperheads, succumb to the venom of internal conflict? Would the state and nation survive? Surely, many thought, the Civil War would bring a radical change. It did bring change. The war's immediate and long-term effects were many, but the basic features of politics and government remained in place. The new party system that developed with the war, for example, was more tightly organized and disciplined, but not fundamentally different from the Whigs and Democrats of the 1830s. More important, despite the intense conflicts of the years 1861–1865 Hoosiers affirmed their attachment to the state and nation, proclaiming vigorously ever after their patriotism and loyalty.

The post–Civil War generation faced a new future in rapid industrialization and urbanization. Fear mixed with hope for a better economic order. Some Hoosiers resisted, arguing that only in small towns and on family farms could fundamental values be preserved. Railroads, factories, and cities might bring efficiency, productivity, and the promise of material prosperity, but they might also bring radical departures in the relations of labor to capital and neighbor to neighbor. Could a Hoosier really be happy working in an auto factory or living in a city? Industrialization and urbanization did bring changes, the most fundamental changes in Indiana's history. Labor strikes led to unions; more visible poverty led to new social welfare agencies; complex economic systems spawned labyrinthian bureaucracies; increased productivity caused a rising standard of living, distributed with considerable inequality. All brought conflict. All required adjustment. Yet the changes were gradual and seldom jarring. Traditions of family and community, which had flourished in pioneer Indiana, held firm through these processes of change.

The economic order that developed by the early twentieth century was volatile and susceptible to crisis, vividly illustrated by the Great Depression of the 1930s. Generating as much fear in Indiana as the economic crisis, however, was the reaction to it by President Franklin D. Roosevelt and Governor Paul V. McNutt. By expanding government's reach into labor-management relations and social welfare Roosevelt and McNutt caused great fear and anxiety. Since the days of the pioneers, many Hoosiers argued, they had taken care of themselves, assisted by family and neighbor but not by government. (This popular argument conveniently ignored many forms of government assistance, beginning in the pioneer period.) Government threatened individual freedom, they asserted. Some, such as Indianapolis businessman Eli Lilly, believed that the nation in the 1930s stood on the brink of destruction and slavery. Roosevelt's "big" New Deal and McNutt's "little" New Deal did push significant liberal reforms onto the state. But the great revolution the Cassandras prophesied never came. Indeed, most historians now regard the New Deal as a force for conserving rather than destroying the American economic and social order. Not only did the New Deal at state and national levels conserve more than it changed, it was followed by a period of very conservative politics in the Hoosier state.

Three challenges—Civil War, industrialization, and New Deal reform—promised fundamental shifts and caused fears that traditional ways and values would be lost in a time of crisis. Such, in fact, was not the case. Some Hoosiers eagerly embraced the new future that was promised, some actively resisted; most took a middle-of-the-road approach. They adjusted, they made compromises and accommodations, they muddled through, all the while seeking to hold to the traditions of the past, to change where necessary but to continue as before where possible. Thus in Indiana's growing cities they attempted to replicate the features of small-town and rural life. Even in Indianapolis, the state's largest city, visitors often commented on the small-town qualities that persisted as the city grew.

Everywhere, family remained dominant, and neighborhood, community, and church continued as central forces in the lives of most Hoosiers. These traditions formed on Indiana's frontier. In clearing fields, planting corn, spinning wool, and cooking johnny cakes pioneers learned how to survive and often to flourish. They worked and lived in tight family units. Beyond the family cabin was the neighborhood of settlements, composed of like-minded pioneers who gathered for worship services, elections, militia drills, and barn raisings. Each claimed independence and autonomy, but each was in fact closely linked to others in a web of economic, social, and political ties—ties that were personal and usually expressed in immediate, first-name recognitions.

This frontier was no utopia. There were economic failures and social misfits, to be sure, but those who persisted developed a special reverence for their beginnings in the new land. In the middle of the nineteenth century they formed "old settlers" associations to celebrate (and sometimes exaggerate) their achievements. Just as the nation celebrated the founding fathers, Hoosiers began to celebrate their founding pioneers. Veneration of those who came first occurred across America, of course, from the New England settlements of the seventeenth century westward across the continent, but Indiana has always been among those places where the hold of the pioneer generation remains most tenacious.

Hoosiers are fortunate to have traditions. In periods of transition healthy traditions take on special importance, providing anchors in the storm. But traditions can also be a drag on a sailing vessel that needs to ride before the storm, threatening to break a mast or causing the ship to founder before reaching a safe harbor. In several areas Indiana's dominant traditions have caused unhappiness that might have been avoided or alleviated by more rapid adjustment to changing winds.

One illustration of tradition's negative effect is race relations. Most white Hoosiers of the early nineteenth century did not extend a neighborly welcome to black Americans. In every area of life Indiana's black people suffered discrimination. Schoolhouse doors were closed to them. So were many churches, hotels, and ballot boxes. In 1851 white Hoosiers went on record in expressing their antipathy to blacks, voting by a five to one margin in a statewide referendum for a provision in the new state constitution that prohibited blacks from settling within the state. Some expressions of hostility were violent, most notably in the mobs that lynched at least twenty blacks in the late nineteenth century. In the 1920s Indiana suffered the national disgrace of an exceedingly popular Ku Klux Klan. The Klan's appeal was broad, emphasizing selected patriotic and Christian values, but appealing to base emotions of racism as well. Less dramatic but as important as the Klan were the many areas of public life that remained closed to black Hoosiers during the first half of the twentieth century. Schools remained segregated in many communities. So were athletic teams, theaters, parks, swimming pools, and public restrooms. Black state legislators sitting in the General Assembly could not eat and sleep in major hotels and restaurants in Indianapolis. And black babies were more than twice as likely as white babies to die before their first birthday. Hoosiers held to their traditions.

Conditions of segregation and discrimination began to change in the middle of the twentieth century. World War II showed some of the practical and ideological stupidities of racism. So did the success of the all-black Crispus Attucks High School basketball team in the 1950s. Indiana was fortunate also in electing a leader in 1960 who rejected traditions of racism. In 1963 Governor Matthew Welsh signed a state civil rights law that marked a new era. Pushed by state and federal laws and by growing voices for tolerance, Hoosiers began to modify old ways. By the 1980s traditional racial epithets, jokes, and forms of discrimination were no longer acceptable. These changes came through evolutionary processes of adjustment rather than radical breaks with the past. Discrimination and inequality persisted, often in subtle forms. As the twentieth century waned Hoosiers clearly had not abandoned entirely one of their most disheartening traditions.

A second illustration of the mixed consequence of persisting traditions is in education. Early nineteenth century Hoosiers never professed goals of racial equality, but they did profess high ideals of education. Indiana's first constitution, written in 1816, promised that the state would create "a general system of education, ascending in a regular gradation, from township schools to state university, wherein tuition shall be gratis, and equally open to all." Such lofty goals were never reached by Hoosier pioneers, who insisted that the necessity of providing for more immediate material needs precluded building a genuine system of free public schools. One logical result was the embarrassing report of the United States census of 1840, which counted only a quarter of Indiana's children between five and fifteen attending school. That same census ranked Indiana last among the northern states in literacy of its adult population.

One consequence of the lag in public education was the state's first school reform movement, begun in the 1840s by Caleb Mills, a Yankee Presbyterian who settled in Crawfordsville. Mills identified the causes of Indiana's backwardness as "want of competent teachers, suitable school books, a proper degree of interest in the community on the subject, adequate funds, and the method of procuring such funds." And Mills concluded, "There is but one way to secure good schools, and that is to pay for them." Such arguments won approval from many Hoosiers, but many others resisted. Education was a luxury, the resisters argued. Schools would cause unbearable tax increases, they predicted. Learning was a mixed blessing at best, they asserted, filling young heads with impractical notions and useless information. Indiana needed more men and women to raise corn, hogs, and babies, not to read books and make speeches.

By the mid-nineteenth century a pattern had been set that would persist to the present. Periodically reports would go forth that Indiana lagged in schooling. Reformers would rise up and make all manner of proposals, nearly all of which would cost money and lead to tax increases. Debate would ensue, with large and loud voices proclaiming that Indiana could not afford to spend one more penny on schools because Hoosiers were already overtaxed. Compromise would result, with slight increases in spending and moderate improvements in the conditions of education. There was no turning point, no break with tradition, but rather a slow, evolutionary process in expanding and improving schools.

Central in the process of change was a growing role for state government compared to local school officials. State laws at the turn of the century made school attendance mandatory and provided some state financial aid to poorer schools. Reformers chipped away at one-room schools, but not until 1959 did they succeed in mandating consolidated schools. Gradually the state assumed more control in finance, curriculum, teacher certification, and other aspects of schooling. Resisters lamented the decline of community influence, the imposition of homogeneous standards from Indianapolis, and especially the higher taxes.

Indiana by the late twentieth century had many good schools and a few that were excellent. But by most measures of educational quality the state lagged behind. Particularly significant was the state's low ranking in per pupil expenditures, especially when compared with per capita income. Indiana was not spending as much of its wealth on education as many other states. Traditions of aversion to taxation and education persisted, even though, as with racism, it may have been less politic to voice such traditions in public.

By the 1980s another round of the periodic outbursts for school reform begun in the 1840s was underway. Perhaps this one would be different, leading to substantial change. Surely more Hoosiers understood that education was the *sine qua non* of the modern world. Surely they could understand the simple fact that Indiana was a relatively prosperous state that did not tax its citizens heavily, that Hoosiers could, if they wished, afford to increase the money and the attention devoted to schools. Surely it bothered them that the best and brightest young men and women were not choosing teaching as a career. Surely they understood that education means not only jobs and material prosperity (the political leaders had hammered home that message) but also that education has significant effect on the quality of life. They knew, didn't they, that life needs to be engaged intellectually and spiritually as well as

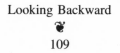
physically. They understood that more Hoosiers needed to have the kinds of educations that would enable them to visit with pleasure the Indianapolis Museum of Art, to read the novels of Booth Tarkington, to understand the prehistoric mysteries of Angel Mounds, the radical hopes preserved in the buildings at New Harmony, the masterful sounds of opera in Bloomington, and, of course, the Japanese business and culture rising in a former cornfield south of Lafayette. And they knew, didn't they, that young Hoosiers had to be able to think about the consequences of acid rain in the air and PCB's in the rivers and lakes; the dangers of drugs and alcohol; the costs of discrimination by race, gender, or age, the choices in presidential elections and in school board elections.

All reformers hope for change. Sensible reformers in Indiana temper that hope with a realistic understanding that there have been no revolutions in the state's past. In education the reforms of the 1980s produced results but no radical breaks with tradition. The sensible reformer will keep pushing, beyond the 1980s, struggling against nearly two centuries of tradition and, with luck, will make moderate improvements.

The traditionalists can look backward to decades of continuity, to the comfort that derives from knowing that revolutionary barricades have never been erected on Hoosier soil. If the past is any guide to the future, the anchors of family, neighborhood, and community will remain central to the quality of life. The streak of independence and individualism that hardened in pioneer times will persist, too. And, of course, basketball will always generate a special fervor.

But times do change, and Hoosiers will change too. They will make some adjustments and accommodations in their traditions. Some of the transitions will be frightening, and some prophets of gloom will predict the end of all that is good and right. But Hoosiers, whether reformers or resisters, need to understand that such a future is unlikely. They will need to think carefully about their traditional ways and beliefs and make hard choices. There is enough good sense in Indiana among reformers and resisters, however, to enable this generation and the next not only to endure but to flourish in the moderate ways that their forebears did. And as they move to the twenty-first century they will be able to continue to smile modestly, to ignore the boastful foolishness from places like California and Texas, and to say quietly, "Ain't God good to Indiana."

NOTES ON CONTRIBUTORS

MARI EVANS

Mari Evans, educator, writer, musician, resides in Indianapolis. Formerly Distinguished Writer and Assistant Professor, ASRC, Cornell University, she has taught at Indiana University, Purdue University, Northwestern University, Washington University, St. Louis, and the State University of New York at Albany over the past seventeen years. She is the author of numerous articles, four children's books, several performed theatre pieces, two musicals, and three volumes of poetry, including *I Am a Black Woman* and *Nightstar*. She edited the highly acclaimed *Black Women Writers (1950–1980): A Critical Evaluation*. Her work has been widely anthologized in collections and text-books.

KAY FRANKLIN

Kay Franklin is a free-lance writer based in Beverly Shores. In the early 1970s, while lobbying for expansion of the Indiana Dunes National Lakeshore, she recognized the significance of the environmental battle still being waged in Indiana. As a result of this experience she coauthored *Duel for the Dunes*, a political history of the long struggle to preserve the dunes. She has also coauthored *Round and About the Dunes*, a guidebook to the area, and has written many articles about the dunes and environs.

TERESA GHILARDUCCI

Teresa Ghilarducci is Assistant Professor of Economics at the University of Notre Dame. She is writing a book, *Labor's Capital: The Economics and Politics of Employer Pensions*, and has published in *Dissent, In These Times, Industrial Relations*, and *Industrial Relations Journal*. She has a Ph.D. in economics from the University of California at Berkeley.

HAL HIGDON

Hal Higdon of Michigan City, Indiana, is a full-time free-lance writer and author of two dozen books, including *Thirty Days in May*, about the Indianapolis 500. He has sold articles to most major magazines and is Contributing Editor for *American Health* and *New Choices* and Senior Writer for *Runner's World*. He has been a competitive long distance runner all his life and has won three world championships in masters (over 40) competition. He also cycles, swims, does triathlons and skis, both downhill and cross country. He and his wife, Rose, a school teacher, have three grown children.

DAVID HOPPE

David Hoppe, Senior Program Officer and Resource Center Director of the Indiana Humanities Council, came to Indiana from California in 1980. He is author of a collection of poems, *Shortest Days,* and a collection of stories about northern Indiana, *Local History*.

JAMES H. MADISON

James H. Madison is a member of the history faculty at Indiana University, Bloomington, where he also serves as editor of the *Indiana Magazine of History*. He is author of *The Indiana Way: A State History* (1986) and *Indiana Through Tradition and Change: A History of the Hoosier State and Its People, 1920–1945* (1982). He has edited a collection of essays, *Heartland: Comparative Histories of the Midwestern States* (1988). His biography of Eli Lilly (1885–1977) will appear in fall, 1989.

MICHAEL MARTONE

Michael Martone was born in 1955 in Fort Wayne. He attended Butler University and graduated from Indiana University in 1977. After working in a Fort Wayne hotel as a night clerk and selling poems in a downtown park during the day, he returned to graduate school in fiction writing at Johns Hopkins University. He has taught writing at Iowa State University. His books of short stories, *Alive and Dead in Indiana* and *Safety Patrol,* as well as his collections of short prose, *At a Loss* and *Return to Powers*, are set in Indiana.

WILLIAM O'ROURKE

William O'Rourke is the author of three novels, *Criminal Tendencies* (1987), *Idle Hands* (1981), and *The Meekness of Isaac* (1974), as well as *The Harrisburg Seven and the New Catholic Left* (1972). He is editor of *On the Job:*

Fiction About Work by Contemporary American Writers (1977) and has received grants from the National Endowment for the Arts and the New York State Council on Arts. He is currently an associate professor at the University of Notre Dame.

SCOTT RUSSELL SANDERS

Reared in the Ohio Valley, Scott Sanders has returned time and again in his dozen books to the landscape of the Midwest. The stories of *Wilderness Plots* (1983) and the historical novel *Bad Man Ballad* (1986) chronicle the frontier epoch of exploration and settlement in the region. The stories of *Fetching the Dead* (1984) and the personal essays of *The Paradise of Bombs* (1987) record his own formative experiences in the Midwest. In *Stone Country* (1985) he examined the quarriers, carvers, landscape, and culture of the southern Indiana limestone belt. At present he is working on a long essay about the Ohio River. While he has traveled widely, the Midwest is the place where he feels most at home, the place he seeks to understand. He teaches at Indiana University in Bloomington, where he lives with his wife and two children.

MICHAEL SCHELLE

Michael Schelle is Composer in Residence at Butler University, Indianapolis. A 1988 Pulitzer Prize nominee for his *Concerto for Two Pianos and Orchestra*, his works have been performed by the Detroit Symphony, the Minnesota Orchestra, Pittsburgh Symphony, Cincinnati Symphony, Orqestra Sinfonica Nacional and the Koenig Ensemble of London. He has won awards from the Barlow Endowment Commission, National Endowment for the Arts, ASCAP, BMI, the Welsh Arts Council of Cardiff, and others.

GEORGE SCHRICKER, JR.

George Schricker is a poet, songwriter, and storyteller who returned to his birth place of Plymouth, Indiana, eleven years ago in order to listen more closely to the voices of the land and his grandparents. He has a particular interest in Native American history and philosophy and has written several ballads concerning the Potawatomi people and their forced removal from the state. Mr. Schricker has worked extensively in Indiana schools and received numerous fellowships for his work with children from the Indiana Arts Commission. In 1987, with the help of his wife, Michele, and son, Ezra, he produced his first cassette of original songs and stories for children, "With Child."

JAMES ALEXANDER THOM

A native of the southern Indiana hills, James Thom returned to his birthplace after a long odyssey in less desirable places. He was a U.S. Marine in Korea, a graduate of Butler University in Indianapolis, a reporter and columnist for the *Indianapolis Star* and The *Fort Lauderdale News*, an editor of the *Saturday Evening Post*, lecturer in the Indiana University School of Journalism, and free lance-writer. His novels are *Spectator Sport* (1978), *Long Knife* (1979), *Follow the River* (1981), *From Sea to Shining Sea* (1984), *Staying Out of Hell* (1985), and *Panther in the Sky* (1989). The author now spends full time researching and writing historical novels and cleaning up after his horses, both occupations requiring patience and hindsight.

MICHAEL WILKERSON

Michael Wilkerson was born in Franklin in 1955. He lives in Bloomington, where he coedited (with Deborah Galyan) a forthcoming anthology of fiction about Indiana. He was the first editor of *Indiana Review*, has published numerous short stories, and is working on a novel about southern Indiana. He is an administrator-teacher at Indiana University.